KU-246-679

.DON COLLEGE

The Hidden Curriculum for Understanding Unstated Rules in Social Situations for Adolescents and Young Adults

**Brenda Smith Myles, PhD,
Melissa L. Trautman, MsEd,
and Ronda L. Schelvan, MsEd**

Foreword by Michelle Garcia Winner

PUBLISHING
P.O. Box 23173
Shawnee Mission, Kansas 66283-0173

20 19004 745

NEW COLLEGE, SWINDON

5405000405662
27th November 2013

PUBLISHING

©2013 AAPC Publishing
P.O. Box 23173
Shawnee Mission, Kansas 66283-0173
www.aapcpublishing.net

All rights reserved. No part of the material protected by this copyright notice may be reproduced or used in any form or by any means, electronic or me- chanical, including photocopying, recording, or by any information storage and retrieval system, without the prior written permission of the copyright owner.

Publisher's Cataloging-in-Publication

Myles, Brenda Smith.

The hidden curriculum for understanding unstated rules in social situations for adolescents and young adults / Brenda Smith Myles, Melissa L. Trautman, and Ronda L. Schelvan ; foreword by Michelle Garcia Winner. -- Rev. and exp. ed. -- Shawnee Mission, Kan. : AAPC Publishing, c2013.

p. ; cm.
ISBN: 978-1-937473-74-7
Rev. ed. of "The hidden curriculum: practical solutions for understanding unstated rules in social situations" / Brenda Smith Myles, Melissa L. Trautman, and Ronda L. Schelvan (Autism Asperger Pub. Co., c2004).
Includes bibliographical references.

1. Autistic people--Life skills guides--Study and teaching. 2. Autism spectrum disorders--Patients--Life skills guides--Study and teaching. 3. Social skills--Study and teaching. 4. Social interaction--Study and teaching. 5. Social learning--Study and teaching. 6. Social skills in adolescence--Study and teaching. 7. Social skills in children--Study and teaching. I. Trautman, Melissa. II. Schelvan, Ronda L., 1952- III. Title.

HM691 .M95 2013   2013932000
371.94--dc23   1302

SWINDON COLLEGE

LEARNING RESOURCE CENTRE

This book is designed in Helvetica Neue.

Printed in the United States of America.

Dedication

We would like to thank the following individuals who contributed hidden curriculum items to this book. Their commitment to individuals with social-cognitive challenges, including autism spectrum disorders, is commendable. This book is dedicated to them.

Jennifer Adair
Carol Affolder
Katie Alexander
Andrea Anderson
Susan Anderson
Aida Ayala-Olivarez
Shana Ayers
Gena Barnhill
Amy Beaver
Judy Becker
Linda Becker
Nicole Benoit
Gayle Bergstrand
Susana Bernad-Ripoll
Shelia Biggs
Cameron Blackwell
Craig Blackwell

Jamie Blackwell
Jen Blackwell
Jordon Blackwell
Patricia Bleish
Monica Bollier
Bobbi Bond
Rhonda Bowen
Dana Bowersock
Megan Brick
Kathy Brodie
Tierney Brown
Erika Buessing
Dawn Bullock
Lisa Burch
Anna Butler
Deborah Byrne
Carrie Calloway

Katherine Campbell
Cindy Carrigan
Rebecca Clark-
   Hermocillo
Annelizabeth Cole
Tina Cole
Janice Cooley
Terri Cooper
Mary Alice Corn
Tina Cornell
Staci Crabtree
Heidi Cromwell
Jennifer Cross
Angie Dalbello
Sandy Davalos
Eileen Davis
Meagan Davis

Karla Dennis
Mary DiMarco
Theresa Duffy
Kathy Delmond
Sarah Dettmer
Kathleen Dewolfe
Lislie Dorrell
Melanie Dunagan
Julia Duval
Marla Eck
Judy Endow
Elaine Fasulo
Heather Ferguson-
  Molino
Kathleen Flinn
Luz Forero
Denise Fraley
Mark Fraley
Shelley Francis
Janet Gertsner
Beverly Gieszelmann
Amanda Gosney
Laura Green
Taku Hagiwara
Sarah Hannibal
Heather Hanzlick
Melanie Harms
June Hayworth
Rebekah Heinrichs
Darlene Hoge
Caren Howes
Anastasia Hubbard
Jill Hudson
Abby Huggins
Rebecca Hughes

Carla Huhtanen
Janice Jenkins
Ketti Johnson-Coffelt
Tyi-Sanna Jones
Candace King
Paul LaCava
Wanda Lee
Jennifer Levenson
Alyssa Linn
Tara Livingston
Robert McCray
Saundra Manley
Stacey Martin
Kerry Mataya
Nancy Michael
Bruce Milford
Nancy Miller
Lisa Mims
Cathy Moseley
Michele Mullendore
Angela Murphy
Erica Neal
Kristine Newcomer
Bridget Newman
Spencer Nolan
Stephany Orr
Hye Ran Park
Mary Peacock
Candace Peters
Bess Powers
Kelly Prestia
Kara Radin
Nicole Rahaim
Jana Rejba
Louann Rinner

Jaime Rivetts
Lisa Robbins
Jacqueline Rogers
Maleia Rome
Mendy Ruthrauff
Jessica Saiter
Susie Sander
Christine Schang
Amy Schapman
Elesa Schmidt
Linda Scott
Rochelle Spicer
Stephanie Stansberry
Lee Stickle
Heather Stoehr
Hsein Su
Jodi Sundquist
Melissa Tate
Kelly Tebbenkamp
Lisa Toler
Shari Walker
Barbara Weatherford
Amy Weed
Jodi White
Shannyn Wilcoxson
Michelle Winburn
Lisa Wimberley
Lori Wood
Annette Wragge
Kathleen Wright
Kelly Yeokum
Amy Zegers
Kristie Ziegler

Table of Contents

Foreword

ocial intuition is the lifeline that saves most of us on a daily basis from an array of potentially disastrous social situations. It also helps us navigate situations that could be physically or mentally harmful. Without realizing it, neurotypical folks constantly, instantaneously and seamlessly survey the unwritten rules or "hidden curriculum" of every environment and every person they encounter to make decisions about how to proceed successfully within a given context. This unconscious social navigator is one of the keys to having good "social skills."

Because good "social skills" generally emerge in neurotypical children with relatively minor effort and minimal coaching from parents and teachers, we take it for granted that all smart people should be able to acquire these naturally. However, within the last 10 years we have begun to acknowledge and explore the fact that there is a group of people who often demonstrate solid to exceptionally strong cognitive and language skills but have difficulties intuiting and adjusting socially to the very sensitive and unstated rules and emotions in everyday environments. These people have "social-cognitive learning disabilities."

This type of learning disability can be confusing to diagnosticians since it tends to encompass a variety of diagnostic labels, including autism spectrum disorders, nonverbal learning disability, attention deficit/hyperactivity disorder, semantic pragmatic disorder, and hyperlexia. It also includes many with Tourette Syndrome, sensory processing disorder, executive functioning challenges, and emotional disturbances, as well as a number of others who have no clear diagnostic label.

Those of us who work closely with persons with social-cognitive learning disabilities recognize that their inability to develop social skills and interpret the social nuances of those around them brings deep and lifelong challenges that impact their lives in a multitude of ways, including socially, emotionally, behaviorally, recreationally and vocationally. It is also important to recognize how personal safety and decision making can be at risk if people are not able to quickly and efficiently adapt to and read social cues and intuit the hidden rules that surround them at every turn.

The good news for people with social-cognitive learning disabilities is that help is on the way! Professionals dedicated to exploring the depth and complexity of what constitutes "social skills" are making tremendous strides in our ability to recognize and develop effective strategies to promote what I refer to as "social thinking." To work with persons with social-cognitive deficits proactively and successfully, educators and parents must be "social anthropologists." For example, on a recent trip to a bookstore, I worked with a client to determine some of the "hidden curriculum" items within the store by exploring how many different sets of rules exist under that one roof. We found that there were at least nine different sets! There were rules to adjust your voice and body as soon as you walk through the doors to enter the store; rules for standing in line at the counter; rules for being in the coffee shop and even more rules for ordering food in the coffee shop; rules for how to behave in the magazine section, children's section, music section, and general book store section; there were even rules for sitting in the section with the big comfy chairs. Thus, to be considered socially appropriate within this one store means that you constantly have to adjust your social behavior to the demands of these "hidden rules." By comparison, imagine how many sets of unwritten rules exist within a school day, for example!

Foreword

This book by Brenda Smith Myles, Melissa Trautman and Ronda Schelvan is a critical tool for helping us all learn more about the hidden social information (e.g., hidden curriculum) that we must analyze in order to be better parents and educators. The analysis provided in the "lists of curriculum items" chapter is just the tip of the iceberg and serves as a jumping-off point for our own analysis of various situations and their social rules. As much as I have thought about the hidden curriculum, this book provides even further food for thought in its exploration of how elusive, dynamic and transient this information is. The gold nugget in this book is that the authors have been able to present complex information in a simple, clear and straightforward way. Thus, it helps us to develop our own frameworks and strategies.

I firmly believe that teaching social thinking and related skills to those who have weaknesses in the intuitive lifelong development of these skills is one of the most complex and challenging things to teach. Breaking down the skills and teaching them step by step as the authors of this book do is the key to success.

Michelle G. Winner, Speech Language Pathologist
Author of *Inside Out: What Makes a Person with Social Cognitive Deficits Tick?*
and *Thinking About You Thinking About Me*

Introduction

The world around us is a complicated place filled with rules, guidelines, regulations, and policies. Although rules and mandates, in themselves, can be complex, most of us take comfort in them – often unconsciously – because they help us to know what to do in most everyday situations. Most of us like rules if they are consistent. It is when they are unclear, are used inconsistently, or are unstated that we become upset, indignant, or confused.

■ ■ ■

Katie entered the ice cream shop with her mother on a hot and humid summer day. She was very excited to get an ice cream sundae to cool off a bit. Katie had been having some difficulty with her parents' divorce lately and was seeing a counselor to talk through some of her concerns.

While waiting in line, Katie spotted her counselor sitting at a table with some other adults. Katie yelled loudly across the ice cream shop, "Hi Mrs. Green!," waving excitedly. As Mrs. Green turned around and waved a quick hello back to Katie, Katie ran towards her and said, "Do these people have problems, too?"

Everyone in the ice cream shop turned around to look at Katie and the adults at the table. Katie then started telling the people at Mrs. Green's table that she was mad that her parents were getting divorced. Her mother ran over to intervene, telling Katie that it was time to go. As her mother rushed her out the door, Katie started crying, not understanding why she had to leave before having a chance to order some ice cream.

■　■　■

Katie didn't understand the unwritten rule that if you see a counselor in a public setting, it isn't appropriate to share information so that others can hear.

We are surrounded on a daily basis by such unstated rules or customs that make the world a confusing place. This is known as the **hidden curriculum**.

The purpose of this book is to make readers aware of the hidden curriculum, its elusiveness, and its impact. Some of us require more instruction in the hidden curriculum than others. Some seem to learn the hidden curriculum or aspects of it almost automatically. Others learn the hidden curriculum only by direct instruction. And that is where this book comes in.

In this second, revised edition of this very popular book, the authors narrow their target to issues common to adolescents and young adults, for whom the social world is already teeming with challenges and uncertainties and who, therefore, need particular support.

Many of the features of the original book have been maintained but important information has been added on evidence-based practice, for example. Also, Chapter Three: Teaching the Hidden Curriculum has been vastly expanded with charts, forms, and templates designed to make the job of teaching and learning the hidden curriculum more effective.

After a general introduction to the nature of the hidden curriculum, a series of instructional strategies will be presented that can be used to teach the hidden curriculum. Finally, extensive, but not comprehensive, lists of hidden curriculum items or unstated guidelines are offered. Due to the elusive nature of the hidden curriculum, the lists – while broad – offer samples rather than a definite set of lessons to be learned. Parents, educators, support persons, and others are encouraged to consider the lists as springboards to making their own lists geared specifically toward the unique needs of the person with whom they are working or living and the given situational contexts.

Chapter One
What Is the "Hidden Curriculum"?

The hidden curriculum refers to the set of rules or guidelines that are often not directly taught but are assumed to be known (Cornbleth, 2011; Garnett, 1984; Hemmings, 2000; Jackson, 1968; Kanpol, 1989; LaVoie, 1994; Myles, Endow, & Mayfield, 2013; Myles & Kolar, 2013). The hidden curriculum contains items that impact social interactions, school performance, and sometimes safety. The hidden curriculum also includes idioms, metaphors, and slang – things most people "just pick up" or learn through observation or subtle cues, including body language. For example, to most a term such as "get off my back" and accompanying body language (frowning, looking irritated, raising voice) communicates that the speaker wants to be left alone, but to somebody who has social-cognitive challenges and predominantly interprets language literally, the term will have a totally different meaning and be very confusing.

If the hidden curriculum is assumed knowledge, you may ask, how can we determine the items that comprise it? This question points to one of the greatest difficulties about the hidden rules – it is difficult to explain all the rules, but when they are broken, they become painfully clear. Therefore, one of the primary ways to recognize an example of the hidden curriculum is when a hidden curriculum error occurs. Certain phrases are indicative that a hidden curriculum item has been violated. For example, if you are ever tempted to make any of the following statements to a loved one, friend, or student, you are probably referring to a hidden curriculum item:

- *I shouldn't have to tell you, but …*
- *It should be obvious that …*
- *Everyone knows that …*
- *Common sense tells us …*
- *No one ever …*

Breaking a hidden curriculum rule can make a person a social outcast or certainly a social misfit. For example, there is a hidden curriculum for nose picking. It is not "do not pick your nose." Rather, it is "pick your nose in the bathroom and use a tissue."

Failure to follow the hidden curriculum can cause a child to be shunned by peers, be viewed as gullible, or considered a troublemaker. Another example of a hidden curriculum item is: "When someone asks, 'do you have the time?' the person does not want a yes or no response; he or she wants to know what time it is at that given moment." The child who unknowingly replies "yes" to this question about time might be punished for purposefully being rude or disruptive. In many cases, the child is neither, but is simply interpreting the question literally.

Teaching the Hidden Curriculum as an Evidence-Based Practice

Three published reports (Centers for Medicare and Medicaid Services [CMS; http://www.impaqint.com/files/4-content/1-6-publications/1-6-2-project-reports/finalasdreport.pdf] 2010; National Autism Center [NAC; http://www.nationalautismcenter.org/pdf/NAC%20Standards%20Report.pdf], 2009; National Professional Development Center on Autism Spectrum Disorders [NPDC on ASD; autismpdc.fpg.unc.edu/content/evidence-based-practices] on ASD, n.d.) have identified evidence-based practices (EBP) for children and youth on the autism spectrum. One of the strategies applies directly to the hidden curriculum. Specifically, the hidden curriculum is an antecedent-based intervention.

An antecedent-based intervention is one that modifies events/ knowledge/skills that typically precede the occurrence of a target behavior. These changes are made to increase success or minimize problems. Much like other antecedent based-interventions (i.e., the Incredible 5-Point Scale [Buron & Curtis, 2012], the Power Card strategy [Gagnon, 2001]), the hidden curriculum is taught to the individual with autism spectrum disorders (ASD) prior to an activity to increase success or decrease the likelihood of challenges. For example, the hidden curriculum for going on a field trip is taught prior to that outing so that opportunities for success are increased

The Elusiveness of the Hidden Curriculum

■ ■ ■

Mary, a 13-year-old on the spectrum, became very upset when she overheard her friend, Julie, talking with another girl, Bailey. She heard Julie speaking in an animated way about something a boy had said to her in class while Bailey said loudly "shut up" several times. Mary become so mad that her friend was being told to shut up that she walked up to Julie and hit her books so hard that they fell to the ground.

Mary didn't understand that "shut up" in this context was a good thing to say. It meant "wow" or "amazing."

■ ■ ■

The hidden curriculum is complex and elusive. Although we have attempted in this book to provide extensive lists of hidden curriculum items, we recognize that it is impossible to identify all such items. What complicates matters further is that you cannot blindly accept all of the hidden curriculum items because many variables come into play in a given situation that influence whether the hidden curriculum item will work for you, a loved one, friend, or student.

For example, the phrase "shut up" can be interpreted in several different ways. When used between two teenage girls engaged in friendly conversation, "shut up" can mean "amazing" or "wow." But between two girls who are angry with each other, the term can mean that the speaker wants the other person to be quiet, to quit talking.

The Hidden Curriculum Differs Across Age

■ ■ ■

Sheldon, from the television series The Big Bang Theory, *often demonstrates hidden curriculum errors. In one episode, Sheldon was at a bookstore looking for a book on how to make friends. He finds a book and sits down at a table next to someone to peruse it. In doing so, he notices that the person next to him is reading a book on a topic that interests Sheldon – monkeys. Sheldon begins to talk with his tablemate about monkeys. The conversation results in sharing names and Sheldon asking his conversation partner if she would like to get together some time.*

It would have been a nice social interaction if his tablemate had been an adult. But she was a 7-year-old child!

■ ■ ■

Another confounding factor about the hidden curriculum is that it changes depending on the ages of the persons involved. The hidden curriculum for a 9-year-old is different from that for a 16- or a 25-year-old. Take, for example, the hidden curriculum item related to getting the attention of someone you like. If you are a 9-year-old boy, you can show that you like a girl by gently pushing her, following her around, pulling her ponytail, or making silly faces.

What if you were a 16-year-old boy and engaged in those behaviors? In all likelihood, you would be instantly ostracized and called "a jerk." Worse yet, if you were 25 years old and did those things, you might be seen as a menace or as potentially dangerous. In fact, it is entirely possible that a 25-year-old in this instance might come to the attention of the police.

Similarly, many children like to play spy games. They eavesdrop on conversations by using mini-microphones and set up play alarms that go off when someone passes them. They also write notes to each other using secret code or invisible ink. This is appropriate at age 9 or 10. At age 18, it could be called stalking.

The Hidden Curriculum Differs Across Gender

■   ■   ■

Terry, a 12-year-old boy with high functioning autism, was the youngest and the only boy in a family of three girls. His older sisters were very protective of him and tried to teach him the hidden curriculum. One of the things his sisters told him was, "Watch what we do and then do the same. On his first day in middle school, Terry decided to follow his sisters' advice. He walked up to a group of guys who were hanging out before school started and said loudly to one of them, "Your hair is so pretty."

He didn't understand why everyone laughed and walked away.

■   ■   ■

While our society has moved toward gender equality and has attempted to do away with gender stereotypes, differences in manner and behavior still exist between males and females. Most of these are not directly taught, but if not understood, they can cause problems and misunderstandings.

The Hidden Curriculum Differs Depending on Who You Are With

■　■　■

Terry's mother, Mrs. Johnson, thought that her son, at age 13, should be taught the hidden curriculum for cursing. Terry had already learned many curse words incidentally and was getting in trouble for using them. His mother considered it natural for 13-year-old kids to curse on occasion and thought her son deserved this rite of passage.

She felt that she could not teach this hidden curriculum item because as a parent her job was to enforce the "no cursing" rule. So she talked with a friend in her neighborhood, Mrs. Smith, who also had a 13-year-old son and asked if her son, Rey, could teach Terry the hidden curriculum rules for cursing. Mrs. Smith agreed that this would be okay. The two mothers sat down with Rey and outlined the most "appropriate" curse words and gave him the hidden curriculum rule for cursing, "Look around first. If you see an adult, don't say any curse words. If you don't see an adult, it is probably okay to use the words in a sentence."

■　■　■

If an adolescent is with an adult, his language is probably not "colorful" and may be somewhat grammatically correct. But if that same adolescent is with his peers (and no adults are in sight), a few curse words might "slip" into the conversation. Is cursing the right thing to do? Of course not, but it is typical of many adolescents, even "good kids."

Does this mean that we should advocate teaching the hidden curriculum for cursing to every adolescent? No! What to teach is an individual decision. Mrs. Smith felt it was the right decision for her son. Other parents may differ, and that is their prerogative.

Cultures Each Have Their Own Hidden Curriculum

■ ■ ■

Brenda had an opportunity to make a presentation in another country. She was the first presenter of the day and was to speak from the stage in a large auditorium. About 20 minutes prior to the presentation, she was on the stage doing last-minute preparations – making sure her computer worked, the projection system was aligned to the screen, the volume was working on the DVD player, and so on. Next to the computer where Brenda was to present stood a chair and a small table that held a pitcher of water and a glass. Having finished checking everything out, Brenda sat down in the chair to wait. Suddenly, an announcement came over the public address system, "Dr. Brenda Myles, please get off the stage."

Confused, Brenda jumped up and quickly ran to sit in the audience. Apparently, she had violated an unwritten rule or protocol dictating that all speakers are to be introduced from the audience and then move to the stage.

■ ■ ■

In some cultures, belching loudly at the end of dinner expresses appreciation for a well-cooked meal. To most of us in the United States, such behavior is considered rude and embarrassing. Similarly, in Italy it is proper for a mother and her adult daughter to walk down the street holding hands. In the United States that behavior would be perceived as odd.

Understanding the hidden curriculum in cultures other than one's own can be difficult. Many cultures have unstated rules involving eye contact, proximity, gestures, and ways of addressing people. Some cultures are high-context cultures, where nonverbal cues are more important than the words that are said. This is significantly different in low-context cultures where words, rather than nonverbal cues, express the real meaning of the conversation.

Reading the Hidden Curriculum of Body Language

Body language is about how we communicate or "speak" with our body. It includes gestures, facial expressions, body posture, and tone of voice. Understanding a person's body language is an important aspect of being able to develop relationships and communicate effectively. Sometimes body language seems different than a person's words, and for this reason, it is important to understand such nonverbal language.

For example, a person who says that he likes you but frowns at the same time might in reality not really like you. A student can often tell if a teacher is angry by the tone of his voice and the way he crosses his arms rather than the words he uses. Sometimes body language is the best way to understand how someone feels. Table 1.1 gives some examples and interpretations of body language.

Table 1.1
Examples of Body Language

Body Part	Action	Visual	Interpretation
Head	Leaning to one side		Not understanding, listening, thinking
Face	Scowl (involves whole face: eyes are narrowed and squinted, nose is wrinkled, lips are pressed together, mouth is sometimes to one side)		Displeasure, intimidation, bullying, anger
Eyes	Wide open		Surprise, amazement
	Almost closed ("open just a slit")		Disbelief, doubt
	Looking straight at someone or something (for longer than a glance)		Staring (which is considered rude)
Eyebrows	Pulled close together (sometimes referred to as "knitted brows")		Thinking, confused
Mouth	Corners of the mouth lifted up (smile)		Greeting, happy
	Corners of the mouth turned down		Sad, unhappy, disappointed
	Opened wide		Surprise, shock

The Hidden Curriculum

Body Part	Action	Visual	Interpretation
Chin	Lifted, pushed forward		Proud, tough, defiant
Body	Pointing a finger		Giving directions, threat, disciplining
	Hands on hips		Frustrated, bored, questioning/ expecting an answer
	Shrugging shoulders		Questioning, unsure
	Arms folded across chest		Unapproachable, listening/ taking in information

18

Chapter Two

The Hidden Curriculum Across Environments

O ften parents, teachers, support staff, and others feel the "hidden curriculum" ideas are primarily for older students and adults, when in fact every age can benefit from instruction pertaining to the hidden curriculum. Understanding the hidden curriculum is essential for all individuals at all ages and in all environments.

While some of the examples in this book may seem somewhat humorous, the impact of not knowing or following the hidden curriculum can be serious. A demonstration of not understanding the hidden curriculum can cause a child to be bullied, ignored, made fun of, or misunderstood. Its impact can be felt in the school, community, home, on the job, or in the judicial system as described below.

School

■ ■ ■

Before school, Mark saunters up to Sam, a third-grade student with ASD and says, "How's it hangin' dog?" Sam gets extremely upset and yells, "I am not a dog!" Mark, who was merely using the latest "in" greeting, shrugs his shoulders and comments to a friend walking with him, "Man, he's weird. Just gonna stay out of his way." Sam, on the other hand, remains unsettled and decides that Mark is a bully.

■ ■ ■

Schools have their own multifaceted hidden curriculum – the unwritten culture of schools. How to dress, what type of backpack to carry, how to greet a fellow student, where to hang out between classes, what games are acceptable to play … the list goes on.

How do students know how to dress? They didn't attend a fashion classes. They learned from observation. They observed the popular kids in school, their heroes in the movies, or studied the catalogues of favorite stores, and drew from these their personal style. Should everyone dress alike? No. Students should be able to express themselves in a manner that is comfortable to them (and within the bounds of school and parental acceptance or tolerance). However, students need to know the hidden curriculum in order to make an informed decision about their appearance.

Within the school, teachers also have their own hidden curriculum – often known as *teacher expectations*. While teachers develop and teach certain classroom rules, they do not teach the many expectations they have for their students. Almost universally, teachers say that they don't teach expectations because they are common sense, are obvious, or should have been taught years earlier. These expectations are the hidden curriculum, and when unstated, they can make school a difficult place for some students.

When children start school, there are many words and phrases that teachers and staff "assume" students know (and understand) when they are being taught routines. Yet, a student who has a limited or narrow focus of vocabulary "pictures" in his head will have difficulty grasping the routine.

■ ■ ■

*Teddy, a first grader with ASD in Ms. Gessler's class, was
sitting on the floor during gathering time. Ms. Gessler was
demonstrating a math problem and asked the children to turn
to their neighbor and whisper the answer. Teddy loudly blurted
out, "But my neighbor isn't here! She was walking her dog
when I left for school." All of the children laughed, and Teddy
was sent back to his desk for disrupting the lesson.*

*Teddy didn't understand the language; he took the teacher's
words literally and put them into the only context he knew. A
simple solution would be for the teacher to say, "When I say
'turn to your neighbor and whisper your answer,' this is what
I mean" (and then demonstrate the action or expectation).*

■ ■ ■

Richard LaVoie (cited in Bieber, 1994) outlined hidden cur-
riculum items that are not understood in the school setting or that
teachers do not address in their classrooms. These include:
- What students should be doing when the bell rings
- Physical plan of the building
- How to travel from class to class in the most direct way
- The administrative structure
- Which administrator is a "safe person" to talk with
- The daily schedule
- The intramural schedule

In brief, what most students "pick up" in the first couple of days
is what should be taught to the students who do not understand
the hidden curriculum, such as …
- Which teachers will tolerate lateness or tardiness?
- Which teachers give homework?
- Which teachers place value on final exams?

Home

■ ■ ■

Margaret has an 11-year-old son, Mark, who has ASD. Although he loves his mother, Mark is not demonstrative – he does not hug her or tell her that he loves her on a regular basis. Because it was important to Margaret that she receive some positive attention from her son, she talked with Mark about the importance of telling parents that they are loved. Mark was flabbergasted that his mother would tell him this, exclaiming, "I told you that I loved you when I was four years old. Why should I repeat myself?" Margaret explained to Mark that mothers generally like to hear frequently that they are loved. When Mark asked for a schedule so that he could tell her on a regular basis, they decided that on every holiday he would say that he loved his mother. Margaret hopes that Mark will become more spontaneous about expressing emotions, but until he does, he at least understands the hidden curriculum rule that parents like to hear often that they are loved.

■ ■ ■

The hidden curriculum at home often is related to the values and rules of the individual family. At other times, it is related to etiquette and tradition. Parents and caretakers often explicitly teach some hidden curriculum items as a typical part of parenting and at other times when they become aware that their children have deficits in these areas. However, these deficits sometimes only become apparent during times of stress and, as a result, children do not receive patient instruction, but instead are given a rule without explanation.

■ ■ ■

Karol is a 9-year-old girl with ASD who has a minor phobia about germs. One day her mother invited a new neighbor who had just moved to New Jersey from Japan to visit. When Sachi Hagiwara, the neighbor, arrived, she immediately took off her shoes. Aghast at this behavior, because her family typically wore shoes in the house, Karol burst out, "Oh, great! We'll probably have to have the carpet cleaned before I can sit on it again." Karol's mother, who was embarrassed by her daughter's outburst, simply told Karol to be quiet.

■ ■ ■

Although her mother's response was typical of what most parents would do in similar circumstances, Karol required more support. She needed explicit instruction on why their visitor took off her shoes and the possible implications for transmitting germs.

Community

■ ■ ■

Twelve-year-old Tom and his mom went to the movie theater to see a new movie based on comic book characters – one of Mark's special interests. As soon as they got there, Mark went into the bathroom – his "pre-show urination ritual." His mom waited outside. Tom's mom was surprised when, after a while, a man came out of the bathroom and asked, "Is that your son in the bathroom? Around 10 or so years old, brown hair, Ramones t-shirt?" "Yes," Tom's mother replied. "Is there something wrong?" The gentleman continued, "I'm a PE teacher, and I thought you should know that your son went into a stall and apparently there was no toilet paper. He came out of the stall with his pants and underwear down and was asking people in the other stalls if they had toilet paper. His junk was just hanging out there. I told him to take another stall and check it first for toilet paper, but I think that he could have easily gotten in trouble in the bathroom. You might want to talk to him."

Tom's mom sighed heavily, thanked the man, and made a note to find out the hidden curriculum for a man's bathroom to share with Tom.

■ ■ ■

While home-related hidden curriculum items are often easily rem-edied by caretakers with little damage to self or others, errors made in the community can have more negative ramifications. Peter Gerhardt (personal communication, April 2004) talks about the hidden curricu-lum of urinals. For example, if there is only one man at a urinal, the hidden curriculum dictates that a newcomer not go to the urinal next to that person. Rather, he should go to a urinal that is at least two stalls away. Also, boys and young men should know that they are not to talk to someone while they are at the urinal and that they should never go to the bathroom in groups. Further, boys and young men should merely unzip to urinate rather than pulling down their pants at the urinal. Boys who pull down their pants could be open to victimiza-tion or be accused of exhibitionism.

On a totally different note, there is a hidden curriculum for going to the library with parents. This hidden curriculum dictates actions in the library as follows:

1. **Why are you at the library?** *To get a book.*
2. **How long are you there?** *Long enough to check out a book.*
3. **How loudly do you talk?** *Talk in a quiet voice or whisper.*
4. **Is it fun?** *It is tolerable, but not particularly fun.*

Parents generally teach this skill to children and youth with social-cognitive challenges, including those with ASD, who often have diffi-culties with the hidden curriculum, and provide careful guidance prior to going to the library and also while at the library. As these children get older, particularly in the middle school grades, they may be invited to the library by peers. The hidden curriculum is different for teens who go to the library, as illustrated below.

1. **Why are you at the library?** *Generally, the excuse is to check out a book or to study; however, it is actually a social activity, a time to hang out with friends, pretend to look at books, talk, laugh.*
2. **How long are you there?** *While parents may want to set a time limit, teens prefer to stay for several hours – until the library closes or they are kicked out.*

3. **How loudly do you talk?** *At the library, the teens talk as loudly as they can without being told to quiet down. It is also likely that loud giggling will occur.*

4. **Is it fun?** *Absolutely.*

Teens who do not know these hidden curriculum rules may be ostracized by peers in the library. In fact, as the teens with ASD follow the former routine: go to their favorite shelf of books, select reading material, announce that they are ready to leave, and prompt their peers to talk more softly.

Dating and other intimate relationships are also surrounded by a hidden curriculum that is very complex. Temple Grandin (1995), an internationally known animal scientist who is on the autism spectrum, has definite views about relationships, "Even today, personal relationships are something I don't really understand … I make social contacts via my work. If a person develops her talents, she will have contacts with people who share her interests" (p. 139). In other words, Temple Grandin recognizes her challenges in this area and has made a deliberate choice to play it safe by staying within the comfort zone of her professional expertise and socializing with people who have similar talents and interests.

Many individuals who have difficulties with the hidden curriculum take a perspective other than Dr. Grandin's and venture beyond the safety of their special interests. If they do, they would do well to learn the specific aspects of the hidden curriculum that involve personal relationships.

Some books that deal with how to develop personal relationships are listed under the heading "Other Materials That Can Be Used to Teach the Hidden Curriculum" in Chapter Four, *Hidden Curriculum Items*. In addition, some basic guidelines are included on pages 33-34 under Social Situations.

Workplace

Many adolescents with autism have employment opportunities while in high school. The importance of these experiences should not be underestimated. Research shows that having paid work experiences while in secondary school is highly correlated with having a job as an adult (Carter, Austin, & Trainor, 2012; Test et al., 2009). Thus, instruction on the hidden curriculum in the workplace should begin when the learner is in middle and high school.

■　■　■

Sixteen-year-old Sonny was participating in a work experience in data entry for XYZ Company. His supervisor, Marcia Johnson, told Sonny that updating the customer database was a priority and that she would provide Sonny with the access code to the database. However, before Ms. Johnson was able to share the access code, she was called into a meeting. When Ms. Johnson came back to Sonny three hours later, she found him sitting at his computer playing Pogo Swing. Ms. Johnson asked, "Why weren't you doing the work in your in-box?" When Sonny replied that he was waiting for the access code, Ms. Johnson told him that he was being terminated.

■　■　■

Mastering the hidden curriculum in the workplace can present major obstacles because adults are assumed to be knowledgeable about workplace mores and, if not immediately competent on these issues, to master them in a short period of time. In other words, there is even less tolerance, and therefore more serious consequences, for breaking curriculum rules in this context.

There are many hidden curriculum items to master in the workplace. For example, it is widely acknowledged in the business literature that two organizational charts exist in every company – one is written up in the company manual; the other, although not printed, is the chain of command that is actually followed. Individuals with social-cognitive challenges and related characteristics, who tend to be very rule-bound, might not discern this difference and, as a result, be ostracized or targeted for not adhering to the accepted chain of command.

Other hidden curriculum issues in the workplace include:

- Can business email be used for personal correspondence?
- What does "casual business dress" mean?
- How do you know when it is timely to introduce a new idea?
- Is there someone at work who should be avoided?
- What is meant by "the customer is always right"?
- What do you do if you disagree with your boss?
- How do you ask for more responsibilities at work?
- How do you negotiate a raise?
- Do you go out to lunch or bring your lunch?
- What does "lunch hour" mean?
- Do you take a break at work? If yes, when, where, and for how long?
- How do you express anger toward a work colleague?

Legal System

■ ■ ■

John, age 22, had never had contact with the police before. Typical of many young adults, John was exceeding the speed limit while driving to work one morning. As a result, he was pulled over by a police officer. The officer approached John, requested that he give him his driver's license, and told him to remain in the car. As the police officer walked back to his car to check John's record for prior violations, John drove off. He did not realize that he was supposed to wait for the officer – merely taking it literally that he was to remain in the car!

■ ■ ■

The hidden curriculum surrounding law enforcement and the legal system is quite complex, and failure to understand or misunderstanding the rules can have severe ramifications.

Recently, an evening news show featured a young man who had been arrested. Obviously distressed, he was sitting in a room with three-way mirrors with a detective. The detective was questioning him – rapidly firing questions at him. At one point, the officer told the young man that if he would confess, he could go home. After only minor deliberation, the young man confessed to the crime, which he had not committed, so that he could go home, as promised. Of course, that scenario did not occur; instead, the young man was incarcerated.

The hidden curriculum items that the young man did not know were many, including:

- Don't confess to a crime you did not commit.
- Call a lawyer if you are being questioned by a law enforcement officer.
- Don't talk to law enforcement professionals until the lawyer is present.

Dennis Debbaudt, in his book *Autism, Advocates, and Law Enforcement Professionals* (2002), offers specific suggestions regarding the legal system for individuals with ASD based on his experiences as a police officer:

> Independent persons [with a social-cognitive challenge] often ask about what they can do when approached by law enforcement professionals. Law enforcers have suggested proper identification, and a prepared handout that includes information that the person has [a social-cognitive challenge] and may not understand their legal rights, explains behaviors that may appear suspicious, and gives any critical medical information and phone numbers for an advocate or law enforcement contact person. Law enforcers also suggest keeping the following in mind:
>
> - Do not attempt to flee.

- Do not make sudden movements.

- Try to remain calm.

- Verbally let the officer know you have [a social-cognitive challenge].

- If unable to answer questions, consider the use of a generic or person specific [a social-cognitive challenge] information card.

- Obtain permission or signal intentions before reaching into coat or pants pocket.

- Ask the officer to contact an advocate, if necessary.

- For the best protection of all involved, the person will either verbally or through an information card invoke the right to remain silent and ask to be represented by an attorney.

- If you are a victim or are reporting a crime, you do not need to have an attorney present to speak to the police, but you may want the police to contact a family member, advocate, or friend who can help you through the interview process. (pp. 101-102)

It is essential that these hidden curriculum items be directly taught to individuals who do not innately understand this system. In addition, more basic information regarding law enforcement is needed. For example, it is critical to understand the cardinal rule not to argue with a police officer even if she is wrong.

Chapter Three

Teaching the Hidden Curriculum

nstruction is key to helping individuals with social-cognitive challenges understand the hidden curriculum as many do not learn these items incidentally. Because of the wide range of hidden curriculum items, it is essential that a variety of instructional strategies be available for educators, therapists, support persons, and parents to use.

The techniques and strategies presented in the following pages provide a structure within which to teach or interpret the meaning of the hidden curriculum.

An Item a Day

The hidden curriculum covers an infinite number of items, so teaching and mastering them can seem overwhelming to teachers and learners alike. By approaching the task based on the saying, "A journey of a 1,000 miles begins with a single step," however, it seems less daunting. Directly teaching one item per day can help students acquire new hidden curriculum information without overloading them and requiring a lot of teacher-student instructional time.

If a teacher begins each day of school by overviewing one hidden curriculum rule and subsequently calling it to the attention of students when she sees it occurring throughout the day, a student can learn 180 items each year. Likewise, if parents present one item each evening as the child is going to bed or during breakfast in the morning, the child can be introduced to 365 additional hidden curriculum examples. Thus, with little effort, children and youth can learn 548 pieces of information a year, which will allow them to be more successful and happier in their home, school, and community.

Some schools have a hidden curriculum item in their school-wide morning announcements and/or dedicate a specific bulletin board for displays of hidden curriculum information. Other schools have students create posters of figurative language/idiom examples and post them in key areas around the school as reminders, and for everyone to see.

Practice Makes Perfect

We believe that the concept of critical mass applies to learning the hidden curriculum. The term is centered around momentum. That is, when there is sufficient momentum in a specific area, that momentum becomes self-sustaining and creates further growth. This idea has been applied to numerous concepts, including knowledge of regular and irregular nouns and verbs (Plunkett & Juola, 1999) and European history (Mazur, 2009). For example, Plunkett and Juola found that when students learned a specific number of noun and verb endings, they were able to generalize that knowledge to regular and irregular nouns and verbs that were not taught to them.

We hypothesize that once individuals with ASD learn a large number of hidden curriculum items (we have yet to define *large number*), their ability to generalize the hidden curriculum, generate new hidden curriculum items, and retain information about the hidden curriculum will increase dramatically. Indeed, the very way they think about the hidden curriculum may change. The hidden curriculum may become an automatic and perhaps subconscious part of the interactions of individuals on the spectrum. Thus, it is important that hidden curriculum instruction be ongoing across environments, people, and situations to ensure that critical mass occurs.

We introduced the concept of critical mass to a noted social worker, author, presenter, and good friend, Judy Endow, who has autism. Judy concurs with our ideas of critical mass and the hidden curriculum, and strongly advocates for inclusion of the hidden curriculum in programs for learners on the spectrum across age, situations, people, and environments. In fact, Judy mentions critical mass in her latest book, *Learning the Hidden Curriculum: The Odyssey of One Autistic Adult* (2012).

Embedding the Hidden Curriculum

As illustrated, there is a hidden curriculum for each environment, for each activity. As such, it is important to understand which hidden curriculum items match a given context. Some models have accurately recognized that because there are hidden curriculum items associated with every environment, every activity should have these items embedded. Three of these models are reviewed here: (a) *Staying in the Game* (Loomis, 2008); (b) *Out and About* (Hudson & Coffin, 2007); and (c) *The Comprehensive Autism Planning System* (Henry & Myles, 2007).

Staying in the Game

Staying in the Game (Loomis, 2008) picks up where many social skills training programs leave off – with generalization. The book addresses this void by presenting a range of interventions aimed at promoting generalization of social skills by showing how to establish social situations that can be opportunities for generalization.

To facilitate generalization, Loomis has identified 10 factors, including the hidden curriculum, that should be considered when programming for social situations (see Figure 3.1). These factors provide the first step in recognizing that a social interaction is more than the sum of its parts (Koenig, De Los Reyes, Cicchetti, Scahill, & Klin, 2009). They vary across events, thus creating challenges that differ dependent on the social event. A brief review of these factors is provided in Table 3.1.

Figure 3.1. Elements of a social situation.

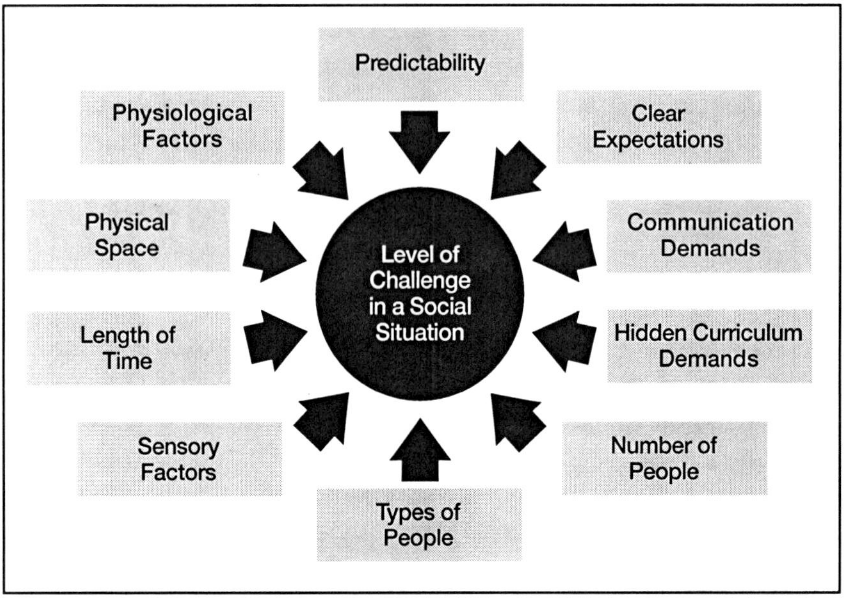

From *Staying in the Game – Providing Social Opportunities for Children and Adolescents with Autism Spectrum Disorders and Other Developmental Disabilities*, by Loomis, J. W. © 2008, p. 19. Shawnee Mission, KS: AAPC Publishing. Reprinted with permission.

Table 3.1

10 Factors That Impact Social Interactions

Factor	Brief Description
Predictability	Routines and regular activities facilitate social success. Activities that are less than predictable can cause anxiety, resulting in the learner's focus being on personal stress experiences rather than social exchanges.
Clear Explanations	Answers to these questions must be provided: Who do you approach? How do you join the activity? When can you talk, sing, yell, etc?
Communication	Verbal and nonverbal communication, emotions, opinions, jokes, and metaphors relative to an activity must be understood.
Hidden Curriculum	Unstated rules, assumptions, and expectations can serve as a roadblock to successful social experiences.
Number of People	The fewer people that are involved, the lower the social challenge.
Types of People	Certain individuals are easier to socialize with than others. It is important, especially in new social situations, to ensure that people who are easy to socialize with are included in activities.
Sensory Demands	All environments have sensory demands, and the majority of individuals with ASD have sensory challenges. A mismatch between the two can cause regulation (typically behavior) problems.
Length of Time	Social processing can be exhausting for learners with ASD. The longer a social event, the more taxing it is.
Physical Space	Crowded spaces, large open areas, noisy environments, and echoing environments can be difficult and/or exhausting for the individual with ASD.
Physiological Factors	Physiological factors, including fatigue, hunger, thirst, and illness can have a negative effect on social interactions.

From *Staying in the Game – Providing Social Opportunities for Children and Adolescents with Autism Spectrum Disorders and Other Developmental Disabilities*, by Loomis, J. W. © 2008, p. 19. Shawnee Mission, KS: AAPC Publishing. Reprinted with permission.

Out and About

Hudson and Coffin (2007), recognizing that every community-based interaction is complex with corresponding hidden curriculum items, developed the Blueprint for community outings in their book, *Out and About: Preparing Children with Autism Spectrum Disorders to Participate in Their Communities.*

The Blueprint is designed to be completed by a caregiver and/or professional who accompanies a child on a community outing and is reviewed with the learner prior to the event. The form's Rewind box (at the bottom) is a place for making notes about what went well and what could be changed or adapted for another similar outing in the future, because even with the best planning, not all outings are successful each time. Figure 3.2 provides a blank template of the Blueprint while Figure 3.3 presents a Blueprint completed for Sebastian, who was invited to a classmate's birthday party.

Figure 3.2. **Blueprint template.**

SUPPORT	STRATEGY	OUTCOME
Waiting Plan		
Communication		
Social		
Visual		
Hidden Curriculum		
Sensory		
Motivation		
Behavior		
Transition		
For siblings or other students		
Additional activities for school		
Additional activities for home		
Rewind		

From *Out and About: Preparing Children With Autism Spectrum Disorders to Participate in Their Communities* by Hudson, J., & Coffin, A. B. © 2007, p. 74. Shawnee Mission, KS: AAPC Publishing. Reprinted with permission.

Figure 3.3. Sebastian's blueprint.

SUPPORT	STRATEGY	DESIRED OUTCOME
Waiting plan		
Communication	Review script of possible questions to ask others and appropriate responses	Holding a conversation on relevant topics with peers
Social	Develop social narrative detailing events of a birthday party	Identifying details and explaining possible choices and reactions
Visual	View pictures of facility decorated for a birthday party	Lessening initial reaction by providing advanced visual warning of environment
Hidden curriculum	Explain how to celebrate the birthday person	Understanding that the majority of attention will go to the birthday person
Sensory	Review possible stimulators: many people, lots of noise; create plan to de-escalate if needed	Recognizing stimulators and take a break before getting too overwhelmed
Motivation		
Behavior		
Transition		
For siblings or other students		

Additional activities for school:

Additional activities for home:

Rewind
Reviewed the social narrative and pictures, identifying good choices that Sebastian made while at the party

From *Out and About: Preparing Children With Autism Spectrum Disorders to Participate in Their Communities* by Hudson, J., & Coffin, A. B. © 2007, p. 49. Shawnee Mission, KS: AAPC Publishing. Reprinted with permission.

The Comprehensive Autism Planning System (CAPS)

The Comprehensive Planning System (CAPS) (Henry & Myles, 2007) is designed to provide an overview of a student's daily schedule by time and activity as well as the supports that the student needs during each period. Following the development of the student's individualized education program (IEP), the educational professionals who work with the student develop the CAPS. Thus, the CAPS allows professionals and parents to answer the all-important question for students with an ASD: What supports does the student need for each activity?

Often referred to as the implementation arm of the IEP, or the "practical IEP" (Aspy & Grossman, 2011), the CAPS (see Figure 3.4) is a list for recording a student's tasks and activities, the times they occur, and the supports needed to support student success. In addition, space is allowed for making notations about data collection and how skills are to be generalized to others settings. Table 3.2 briefly describes each of the CAPS components. Figure 3.5 provides an example of two activities (Priming at 8:00 a.m. and Review of Day at 3:00 p.m.) that occur during the school day for Jye, an 8-year-old on the spectrum. A hidden curriculum idea of the day is presented during the first activity and reviewed during the last activity.

Figure 3.4. Blank CAPS form.

Comprehensive Autism Planning System (CAPS)

Child/Student: _____

*ss=state standard

Time	Activity	Targeted Skills to Teach	Structure/ Modifica- tions	Reinforce- ment	Sensory Strategies	Communica- tion/ Social Skills	Data Collection	Generalization Plan

From *The Comprehensive Autism Planning System (CAPS) for Individuals With Asperger Syndrome, Autism, and Related Disabilities* by Henry, S. A., & Myles, B. S. © 2007, p. 216. Shawnee Mission, KS: AAPC Publishing. Reprinted with permission.

Table 3.2
Items on the CAPS

CAPS Category	Brief Description
Time	This section indicates the clock time when each activity takes place that the student engages in throughout the day.
Activity	Activities include *all* tasks and activities throughout the day in which the student requires support. Academic periods (e.g., reading, math), nonacademic times (e.g., recess, lunch), and transitions between classes are all considered activities.
Targeted Skills to Teach	This may include IEP goals, state standards, common core standards, hidden curriculum items, and/or general skills that lead to school success.
Structure/ Modifications	This can encompass a wide variety of supports, including placement in the classroom, visual supports (e.g., choice boards, visual schedules), peer supports (e.g., Circle of Friends, peer buddies), and instructional strategies (e.g., priming, self-monitoring).
Reinforcement	Student access to specific types of reinforcement as well as a reinforcement schedule is listed here.
Sensory Strategies	Sensory supports and strategies identified by an occupational therapist are listed in this CAPS area.
Communication/ Social Skills	Specific communication goals or activities as well as supports are delineated here. Goals or activities may include (a) requesting help, (b) taking turns in conversation, or (c) protesting appropriately. Supports, which are also diverse, may encompass (a) language boards; (b) PECS (Picture Exchange Communication Systems; Frost & Bondy, 2002); or (c) other augmentative communication systems.
Data Collection	Data collection includes gathering information on behavior(s) to be documented during a specific activity. Typically, information in this section relates to IEP goals and objectives, behavioral issues, and state standards.
Generalization Plan	Because individuals with ASD often have problems generalizing information across settings, this section of the CAPS was developed to ensure that generalization of skills is built into the child's program.

From *The Comprehensive Autism Planning System (CAPS) for Individuals With Asperger Syndrome, Autism, and Related Disabilities* by Henry, S. A., & Myles, B. S. © 2007. Shawnee Mission, KS: AAPC Publishing. Reprinted with permission.

Figure 3.5. Jye's CAPS for priming and end of the day review.

Comprehensive Autism Planning System (CAPS)

*ss=state standard

Child/Student: _____

Time	Activity	Targeted Skills to Teach	Structure/ Modifications	Reinforcement	Sensory Strategies	Communica- tion/ Social Skills	Data Collection	Generalization Plan
8:00	Priming (with small group)	Hidden curriculum item of the day, Identifying emotions, Managing stress	Visual schedule, Mindreading software, Social narrative on anxiety, Quiet area, as needed	Reinforcement menu	Incredible 5-Point Scale of Sensory Needs	Hidden curriculum/ multiple meanings list, Emotions notebook, Change card	Emotion recognition (software takes data), Meltdowns (#, daily)	Visual schedule, Social narrative on anxiety
3:00	Review of day							

41

Other Materials That Can Be Used to Teach the Hidden Curriculum

The ideas presented in this book can be supplemented with other materials that address issues surrounding the hidden curriculum. The following is a brief list of books that may be used to teach children and adolescents unwritten rules. Parents and teachers may want to preview the books before using them to ensure they teach the hidden curriculum items you want your children and students to know.

The Hidden Curriculum and Other Practical Solutions to Everyday Challenges for Elementary-Age Children With High-functioning Autism Spectrum Disorders, 2nd ed. (Myles & Kolar, 2013). Written specifically for children with ASD ages 5-11, this practical book covers many of the innumerable everyday occurrences that can complicate the lives of children with ASD. The following sections are particularly relevant: school-related, getting along, emotions and concerns, and miscellaneous.

How Rude! The Teenager's Guide to Good Manners, Proper Behavior, and Not Grossing People Out (Packer, 1997). This book covers everything from getting along with peers to using "netiquette" (online etiquette). The book is fast-paced, entertaining, and written in teenager-friendly language.

A Little Book of Manners for Boys (Barnes & Barnes, 2000). In this book Coach Bob talks to boys about being a good sport, taking care of things, eating, and other important issues. The book is written for boys between the ages of 6 to 12. Parents can read one item per day to a child and discuss it at the dinner table or at bedtime.

A Little Book of Manners: Courtesy and Kindness for Young Ladies (Barnes, 1998). This colorful book features Aunt Evelyn and Emilie, who discuss telephone, mealtime, playtime, and visiting manners, among other topics. The book is structured as a series of short vignettes that can be read by or to a child.

The American Girl series by Pleasant Company. This series of books is invaluable to girls of all ages. The books feature lifelike, attractive illustrations and use language that is informal, but informative. Books in the series include *The Care and Keeping of You: The Body Book for Girls* (Schaefer, 1998), *I Can Do Anything: Smart Cards for Strong Girls* (Kauchak, 2002), *Writing Smarts: A Girl's Guide to Writing Great Poetry, Stories, School Reports, and More!* (Madden, 2002), *The Feelings Book: The Care and Keeping of Your Emotions* (Madison, 2002), and *Staying Home Alone: A Girl's Guide to Feeling Safe and Having Fun* (Raymer, 2002).

Life Lists for Teens (Espeland, 2003). This book is a great resource for teens of all ages. It covers an extensive array of topics about life experiences, how to get along, learn and have fun.

Summary

This chapter highlighted the importance of teaching the hidden curriculum and the concept of critical mass, which posits that sufficient instruction is needed so that the learner has adequate knowledge to begin to understand the hidden curriculum independently. Generalization is also enhanced when the hidden curriculum is embedded into everyday activities. Using the *Staying in the Game* template, *Out and About* template, and the *Comprehensive Autism Planning System (CAPS)* can help facilitate instruction and critical mass. Other resources for hidden curriculum information were also presented.

Chapter Four

Hidden Curriculum Items

While we recognize that it is impossible to identify all of the hidden curriculum items that lead to life success, on pages 47-94 we have compiled lists that will be useful as you plan formal instruction. We hope that reading these items will help you to identify others that may be essential to children and youth who don't innately understand the hidden curriculum.

Readers need to keep in mind that the hidden curriculum items presented here are general guidelines of what to do or what not to do. As discussed earlier, they may differ based on who you are with, where you are, the interpretation or perspective of those involved, and so on. It is always a good idea for those learning the hidden curriculum to discuss these items with adults they trust. The hidden curriculum items are organized around the following major topics:

- Airplane Trips
- Bathroom Rules
- Behavior in Public
- Birthday Parties

- Clothing
- Dangerous Situations
- Eating
- Friendship
- Grocery Store
- Holidays
- Home Life
- Life Activities
- Medical Appointments
- Movie Theaters
- Neighbors
- Pets
- Religious Services/Funerals
- School
- Social Interactions
- Social Networking
- Sporting Events
- At the Swimming Pool
- Texting/Cell Phones/Emails
- Vacations
- Video Games/Arcades
- Figurative Speech and Idioms
- Slang Terms

Hidden Curriculum Items: Airplane Trips

- When going to the airport, it is important to follow the directions of the airline staff. Yelling or arguing with them can get you in trouble.

- If you have an item that you want to take on a plane with you, remember to take it out of your suitcase before you check in your luggage with the airline.

- At the airport, you may have to park in a parking lot far away. You may need to wait for a short period of time before a shuttle bus picks you up and takes you to the terminal.

- When riding on an airplane, use only one armrest. If you are sitting in an aisle seat, it is usually best to use the armrest on the aisle side.

- Avoid placing any part of your body over the armrest and into another's seating area.

- Soft drinks and snacks are usually free on airplanes.

- Do quiet and sedentary activities during the flight (reading, computer, writing, etc.).

- If you are playing a video game or MP3 player/iPod/iPad, turn the audio volume off or wear headphones. Make sure that your MP3 player, iPod, etc., is powered up before the flight.

- The temperature on an airplane may not be comfortable for you. Think about wearing or bringing a lightweight shirt and jacket/sweatshirt.

- When listening to music, sing quietly to yourself, not out loud.

- Unless you are in the aisle seat, try to limit the number of times you leave your seat.

- Airlines usually don't provide a variety of food during a flight. It is best to bring a small snack if you think you will get hungry and have specific tastes.

- Don't tell the person sitting next to you that he is too fat for the seat.

- When sitting in your seat, don't push, pull, or kick the seat in front of you.

- Sit in your seat facing forward, not backward, regardless of who is sitting behind you.

- Remember to keep your feet on the floor and not on the back of the seat in front of you.

- Never joke about carrying guns, knives or bombs when at the airport or on the plane.

- Sometimes airplanes are not on schedule. The only thing that you can do is to calmly accept the change.

- If the airplane you are on temporarily has to stay parked on the runway, do a quiet activity to help pass the time.

Hidden Curriculum Items: Bathroom Rules

- When you are in a public restroom, talking above a whisper can be heard by people outside the stall. Make sure what you are talking about is O.K. for everyone to hear.

- Sometimes people accidentally turn the lights off when they leave the bathroom. If you are in the bathroom and someone turns the lights off, it's O.K. to "yell" nicely for someone to turn them back on.

- Always wash your hands after you use the restroom.

- Make sure that you flush the toilet after you use it.

- Always close the door when using the restroom.

- When using the toilet, go in the toilet, not on the toilet. If you go on the toilet by mistake, wipe the toilet seat with unused toilet paper.

- Pull up your pants before coming out of the stall.

- Don't talk about what you did in the bathroom.

- For girls: Learn which toilets you can sit on and which toilets are better to squat over, or use a paper seat cover. It is generally a good idea to squat over or place a paper seat cover on toilets in public places or those that don't appear clean.

- For boys: Don't talk to others around you when using the bathroom.

- For boys: When using the urinal, instead of pulling your pants down, just unzip them, pull out your penis, urinate and put your penis back in your pants and zip them up.

- For girls: Don't talk to the person in the next stall, unless she is a friend of yours.

- When entering the bathroom, don't look through the separations between the stall doors to see if a stall is empty. Look under the stall door, towards the bottom of the toilet. If you see someone's feet, use a different stall.

- Don't write on the bathroom walls (even if others do).

- Avoid complaining to the person who just came out of the bathroom that she made it stink.

Hidden Curriculum Items: Behavior in Public

- If you see someone in a wheelchair, don't stare. Staring can make the person feel uncomfortable.

- When out in the community, hold doors open for someone older than you or when someone is close behind you.

- In the community, if you see someone smoking, refrain from yelling "Second Hand Smoke Kills!"

- Even if you are really upset, never say something threatening in public, especially not about hurting someone or blowing something up. Someone might think you are serious and call the police.

- Don't make threats when you are upset. Threats, especially if they involve violence, can be taken seriously and get you in trouble. Instead, let the person know you are upset and need to be left alone.

- Be on your best behavior when in public.

- If you are in public and have a meltdown, don't yell things like "You're hurting me!" or "Help me!" at the person trying to help you. Bystanders might not understand and call the police because they think someone is trying to hurt you.

- If you are walking with others, it is a good idea to walk beside them if there is enough room. Walking in front of somebody can seem cocky, and walking behind can make the person feel as if you don't want to be seen with him.

- Walk with your hands down to your side.

- Sometimes we have to walk quickly, but sometimes it is O.K. to go slow.

- If you have to get past someone, say, "Excuse me." Don't push people out of the way.

Hidden Curriculum Items: Birthday Parties

Before the Party

- If everyone in your family is busy cleaning the house for a party, help out, too. It could frustrate your siblings or parents if you sat around and watched them clean.
- Don't ask to be invited to someone's party.
- The birthday party may not be celebrated on the actual day of the birthday.
- If you are around people who are not invited to a party, don't discuss plans for the party around them.
- Buy a present for the person that he would like – not something that you would like.

At the Party

- The host/birthday girl or boy is the "boss."
- If you are a teenager and the party is an all-girl party, the topic of conversation may be about boys.
- You may not like the theme of the birthday party – people have different interests and tastes. If you don't like the theme, don't tell the host.
- While you are at a birthday party, avoid talking about your last birthday party and how much better it was.

The Birthday Cake

- Only the birthday person can blow out her candles, unless she invites somebody to help out.
- You may not like the design on the cake, but don't say that the cake is ugly.
- If you don't like the flavor of the cake, you may simply say, "No thanks" or "I don't care for any right now" when offered a piece.
- Wait until the birthday person blows out the candles and the cake is cut before you eat a piece of cake.
- If the birthday person is older, there will be many candles on the cake. Refrain from saying things like "The cake is as bright as the sun" or "I need my sunglasses."
- Sometimes you may not like all of the food that is offered at the party. Don't tell the host that the food is bad. In declining, just say, "Maybe I'll eat something later," "Not right now, thank you," or "I am not hungry right now."

Hidden Curriculum Items: Birthday Parties (cont.)

Gifts

- When you are invited to a birthday party, you are expected to bring a wrapped present with a card unless the invitation says not to bring gifts.

- The person whose birthday it is gets to unwrap the presents by himself.

- Don't announce how much the present costs.

- Only the person who receives the present can play with the present, unless she gives you permission.

- Don't make rude comments about the gifts others gave the birthday person.

- When you give a gift that you had previously owned to someone, don't tell her that you did not want it any more.

- Refrain from telling someone you don't like his gifts.

- If you get a present that you already have, don't say, "Oh, I've already got five of these. Where can I take it back?" Instead, you can say something like, "This is a great gift – it is so good that I already have one." You can exchange it later.

- If you know what a person is getting for his birthday, don't tell him. Just say that you cannot share that information because it is a secret. It is not a lie to keep this kind of information secret.

Hidden Curriculum Items: Clothing

- If you tend to wear a certain brand of clothing, remember that not everyone has to wear that same brand.
- At school, most students wear different outfits every day.
- It is a good idea to check the weather before you get dressed so you know what to wear. But remember that the weather forecast is not always totally accurate.
- Pajamas should not be worn outdoors.
- When you are out in public, a proper place to fix undergarments is in the bathroom stall. Don't pull on your underwear to "fix" them unless you are in the bathroom or another private place. Also, don't adjust your private parts in public.
- Untie your shoes before you try to put them on.
- It is inappropriate to take your clothes off in public even if you are hot.
- It is inappropriate to take your jeans off at school even if you are really hot or the jeans are uncomfortable
- It is not cool for boys to wear pink underwear.
- Don't wear clothes so tight that people can see the line of your underwear through your clothes.

Hidden Curriculum Items: Dangerous Situations

- Remove cords from electrical sockets by holding the plug and pulling gently.
- Never agree to meet someone who has only contacted you on the Internet without your parents' knowledge. There are adults who pretend to be younger in order to meet children and teens, and those kinds of people can be dangerous.
- If you are walking down a street or in a parking lot, you may see an area sectioned off with yellow caution tape. Make sure to stay away from that area; it can be dangerous.

Hidden Curriculum Items: Eating

Basic Rules

- Don't sample food and lick your fingers while you are serving yourself. That can spread germs and gross out others who are eating from the same food.

- Never put anything you find on the ground in your mouth.

- "Double-dipping" (dipping again after you have taken a bite) your chips or other food into the dip is not O.K. unless you have your own private bowl. It is unsanitary.

- Wash your hands before eating meals and snacks.

- Always chew your food with your mouth closed.

- Put your napkin on your lap, not under your chin.

- Don't eat someone's food without asking.

- Use your own utensils to eat with – don't grab utensils from another person's plate.

- Use a tissue, not your napkin, to blow your nose.

- Don't blow your nose at the table. Excuse yourself and go to the bathroom to blow your nose.

- If you have to cough or sneeze, cover your mouth and move your head a little bit away from the table. When finished, wrap the tissue and put it in your pocket, then say, "excuse me."

- After eating, refrain from leaning back in your chair and rubbing your stomach.

- Don't put ketchup or other condiments on everything you eat. This may gross out other people, and they may not want to sit by you next time.

- Don't brush your hair at the dining table.

- Keep food in your mouth at all times. Avoid taking a bite of food and spitting it back onto the plate, even if you don't like it.

- Burping out loud is not appropriate when eating.

- Use your own cup when you want a drink – don't drink out of a cup that is not yours.

- "Zapping" or "nuking" something means to heat it up in the microwave, not blowing something up with an atomic bomb.

Hidden Curriculum Items: Eating (cont.)

Buffet Lines

- Get a clean plate for each trip you make to the buffet.

- Never touch food on the buffet with your hands.

- If you drop something at the buffet table, leave it there.

- Wait until you sit down at your table before you start eating your food.

- Remember to use your fork and spoon, and possibly knife.

- Always use a napkin to wipe your face and hands, especially before you make a second trip through the buffet line and before you leave the restaurant.

Eating at Fast-Food Restaurants

- Fast-food restaurants may have indoor play areas. Most of these play areas have height and weight limits. Make sure to check the requirements before playing in the play area.

- Don't wait to be seated at a fast-food restaurant.

- Wait in line to place your order.

- Learn how to order something in a fast-food restaurant.

- People have to clean their own tables and throw away their own trash at fast-food restaurants.

- When you get carryout food, don't turn the container of food on its side or upside down as the food may spill out.

Eating at a Friend's House

- If you are visiting someone's home, it is not O.K. to go through the cabinets looking for food. If you are hungry, ask if you may have a snack or wait until a meal is served.

- When eating at a friend's home, wait until the head of the house says the food is ready. Don't go to the kitchen to see what is for dinner and ask when the food is going to be ready.

- Eat what you are served if there are no choices. If you don't like what is being served, say, "Just a little bit, please; I'm not very hungry" instead of "I don't want anything – I don't like it."

- If the host offers more and you are full or don't like the food, say, "No thank you, I'm fine," instead of "It was disgusting."

- When asked, "How is your meal?" be polite even if you did not like the food. It is kind to say, "Thank you for cooking such a nice meal" or "Thanks for inviting me to dinner."

- Know what the rule is for leaving the table. In some homes, a child may not leave the table until the head of the family is finished eating and leaves the table. In other families, a child may ask to be excused when he is finished eating. It is O.K. to ask the adults what the rule is.

Hidden Curriculum Items: Eating (cont.)

Eating at a "Sit-Down" Restaurant

- Sometimes you have to wait for a table at a restaurant. The hostess will do her best to estimate how long the wait will be, but it may take longer than what she first said.

- When you are sitting at a restaurant, keep your legs and feet under the table so you don't accidentally trip someone walking by.

- When you are in a restaurant, don't lean over the booth to look at the people behind you. Respect their privacy and stay in your seat.

- Don't bring food from one restaurant into another restaurant.

- If you're in a restaurant, don't talk out loud about how much you prefer a competing restaurant.

- It is rude to slurp loudly the last bit of your drink through your straw.

- If your mouth is full of food when it is your turn to talk or respond, you can hold up your pointer finger to request a minute before answering.

- If you don't like your food in a restaurant, don't complain loudly. Just quietly let the server know and ask if it can be fixed or if you can get something else.

- When you are eating at a restaurant, it is not polite to comment on conversations going on at other tables. You may overhear what other people are saying, but they are not talking to you.

- When eating out, excuse yourself politely to go to the bathroom. You may have to ask the waitress where the bathrooms are.

- Learn about the dress code before going to a fancy restaurant. Don't wear jeans to a fancy restaurant.

- Refrain from talking about other people sitting next to you – don't comment on what they are eating or drinking, or what they look like.

- Use a quiet voice in the restaurant. You don't have to whisper – just talk in a low-volume voice.

- Don't start eating until everyone has been served. When everybody else at your table starts eating, you may start.

- If finished eating, wait patiently for the others at your table to finish.

- Take small bites and eat slowly.

- When you are in a nice restaurant, conversation should not include stories that contain the word "blood" or stories that might be considered to be gross or gory.

- Don't ask anyone preparing the food in a public place when the food inspector is coming to check the kitchen.

- Don't tell the waitress that her hair is messed up.

- When eating out, place your napkin on your lap or keep it on the table.

- Appetizers are a part of the meal that people typically share. Don't eat all of the food on the appetizer plate. Make sure everyone who wants some gets some.

- When leaving the restaurant, never pick up money left on the table.

Hidden Curriculum Items: Eating (cont.)

Miscellaneous Eating-Related Rules

- When eating in a group, but not at a restaurant, it is polite to offer someone else some of your food or drink if you have enough.

- At the grocery store, it is O.K. to eat food when someone offers you something to try as part of a sample or taste test. If it is a sample or taste test, just try one piece. You cannot just try anything that you want without paying for it.

- Only take small helpings of food when eating "family style." Allow everyone to eat at least one serving before you help yourself to all of one item.

- If you are making a shake with a blender, make sure that there are no objects in the blender (like a spoon). Also, make sure the lid is on tight.

Hidden Curriculum Items: Friendship

Borrowing From a Friend

- Take care of other people's property as well as you take care of your own – perhaps even better than your own.

- When you borrow a book or CD from somebody, take good care of it and return it in the same condition as when you borrowed it.

Building and Keeping a Friendship

- It is O.K. to have different opinions than your friend. Sometimes friends don't agree with one another. It does not mean that one person's opinion is better than the other's.

- Real friends share their secrets and dreams with each other. Don't share your private thoughts with everybody you meet. It takes time to develop the kind of trust true friends have.

- Friends don't constantly make negative comments to each other.

- If a friend cancels plans with you, it is not appropriate to repeatedly ask why. Sometimes things come up and plans change.

- If you can't hear what a friend is saying, just kindly ask him to repeat it.

- If someone asks you to lie, say firmly that you will not do it. Friends never tell each other to lie.

- If you accidentally break something that belongs to a friend, be honest. Tell your friend what happened and that you're sorry. Then offer to replace what you broke if it cannot be fixed.

- If you are with a group of friends and you have candy or gum to share, make sure you have enough for everyone so no one is left out.

- If you have something that is really special to you and that you don't want to share, put it away when you have a friend over to play.

- When you have a friend over to play, it is polite to let your friend choose an activity first. Then you can pick something to do for the next activity.

- It is not polite to tell a friend that you like another friend better than her.

- You should not have to buy gifts for or give money to your friends to keep them as friends.

- When your friend is telling you about something she is really excited about but you aren't, try to be excited about it while she is talking to you. Otherwise, she will be disappointed and will probably stop talking with you.

- Sometimes after you have made plans with a friend, something else comes along that you would rather do. It is not O.K. to drop the first plan just because you would rather do the second.

- If a friend holds his fist out in front of you, he may want to bump his fist against your fist, which is like giving a "high 5." Just gently bump your fist on his fist in response.

Hidden Curriculum Items: Friendship (cont.)

Building and Keeping a Friendship (cont.)

- If you and your friend both want the last piece of cake, one solution is for one of you to cut it in two and then each take a piece. The person who cuts the cake waits for the other person to take her piece.

- If a friend offers you a piece of gum or candy and you don't care for the flavor, just politely say, "No, thank you." Don't make a big deal out of it.

- Friends tell each other secrets and their likes and dislikes. Friendship is different from just meeting someone on the street and talking to them.

- Friends say nice things to each other, not nasty comments like "You are fat."

- It is O.K. to be mad at your friend sometimes. Tell you friend politely that what he did made you mad and try to work out your differences. Sometimes it is O.K. "to agree to disagree."

- Friends forgive each other for mistakes they accidentally make.

- Friendship takes a lot of time to develop. Just because someone in your class was nice to you one time, it does not mean that he or she is your best friend.

- You should not have to pay somebody to be your friend.

- If someone never asks you to play, it is probably not a good idea to ask him to play every day.

- When you want to play with someone, don't pressure or nag at her if she tells you she cannot play.

- Don't play in other people's backyards unless you are invited.

- Just because a person is very popular, it does not mean that he is nice or a good person to have as a friend.

- When you are getting to know someone and want to invite the person to your house, consider doing a structured activity first, such as going to a movie or playing mini-golf. With these types of activities, there is a definite starting and ending time and you don't have a lot of time to talk.

- When you invite someone over to your house, you can alternate what you both want to do. For example, you can both do something that your guest wants to do first, and then you can both do what you want to do.

Visiting a Friend's House

- Always wipe your feet before entering somebody's home, especially if it is rainy or wet outside.

- When you walk up to or past someone's house, don't look in through the windows or doors.

- If you are knocking on the door or ringing the doorbell and nobody answers the door, leave and come back later. Don't let yourself in even if the door is open or unlocked.

Hidden Curriculum Items: Friendship (cont.)

Visiting a Friend's House (cont.)

- If you are at a friend's house and she has a toy you really like, it is not O.K. to take the toy home with you. It belongs to your friend, and if you steal she won't want to be your friend.

- Don't invite yourself to someone's house. Wait for an invitation.

- When you are riding in a friend's car with a DVD player, it's polite to let your friend choose the movie, even if you don't like the movie he chooses.

- Your friends may not have the same television channels you do. It is not O.K. to order new ones on their television without asking. Pressing buttons on their remote may cause problems with their television.

- If you spill a drink at a friend's house, ask your friend or the adult in charge for something to clean it up with. Say you are sorry, and then clean up the spill the best you can.

- When you enter someone's home and you see shoes by the door, it usually means that the family has a rule of not wearing shoes in the house. If you are not sure, ask, and then follow the house rules.

- When you meet your friend's parents for the first time, don't tell them about problems you are having or secret things you did with your friend.

- When you go to someone's house, don't kick off your shoes, lie on the couch, or help yourself to food from the refrigerator unless you have been told by the people there that you may.

- Try not to ask your parents if a friend can stay for supper in front of your friend. It is embarrassing to both the friend and your parents if they say no.

Staying Overnight

- If you sleep over at a friend's house, you may not always be on a bed and you may not be sleeping in an area by yourself.

- When you spend the night with someone, you should follow her routine, not your normal home routine. It is O.K. to ask her questions if you are not sure of what to do.

Hidden Curriculum Items: Grocery Store

- When you are in line to check out at the store, don't comment on how much people in front of you spend and don't stand too close as they pay.

- When standing in line at the grocery store, it is acceptable to carefully look through the magazines while you wait. However, it is not O.K. to try to finish looking through the entire magazine while others are waiting in line behind you.

- Don't tell the man at the grocery store that he is big and fat even if you think he is.

- At the grocery store, it is O.K. to eat food when someone offers you something to try as part of a sample or taste test. If it is a sample or taste test, just try one piece. You cannot just try anything that you want without paying for it.

- If there is long line at the store, try to be patient. It's usually not helpful to yell for the manager.

- An express line at the grocery store usually has a sign that tells you how many items that you can check out at one time. If you are in an express line and the person in front of you has more items than allowed, it is best just to ignore it.

Hidden Curriculum Items: Holidays

- Different people celebrate different holidays for different reasons. It is polite to ask about a person's celebrations and traditions with respect.

- Families have different traditions during holiday seasons. If a friend invites you to join her family tradition and it is different from yours, accept if it feels comfortable or politely thank her for the invitation if you decline.

New Year's

- New Year's Eve is a celebration of the upcoming year. It's a tradition to stay up to watch the time wind down until midnight.

- People often make "resolutions" at the beginning of a new year. These are goals for things they want to accomplish. It is impolite to suggest to somebody that she ought to make a resolution to lose weight.

- When your parents or teachers are writing down the New Year (e.g., 2013), they may accidentally write the previous year. A lot of people make this mistake at the beginning of the new year.

Groundhog's Day

- "The groundhog saw his shadow" refers to a traditional way of predicting that winter will last for another six weeks. It is not an exact or reliable way to forecast the weather, however.

Valentine's Day

- In elementary school, if your class has a Valentine exchange, you are supposed to bring a Valentine's card for each student in your class, otherwise someone might feel left out.

- Valentine's Day is a good time to tell your family that you love them. This may be your mother, father, grandmother or other family members. Just because it's Valentine's Day, it doesn't mean that you tell someone you like at school that you love him or her.

- If you receive a Valentine's Day card from another classmate that says, "Will you be mine?" it does not mean that he or she wants to be your boyfriend or girlfriend.

St. Patrick's Day

- It's a tradition on St. Patrick's Day to wear green. Because it is a fun tradition, if someone does not have green in their clothing, they may be pinched lightly by another person.

- On St. Patrick's Day, if you see someone of short stature and wearing green, they are not a leprechaun. They won't think it's funny if you ask them if they are.

April Fool's Day

- On April Fool's Day, people may play practical jokes on others. If someone plays a practical joke on you, try not to become upset or frustrated. Talk to an adult if you feel the joke is mean or upsets you.

Hidden Curriculum Items: Holidays (cont.)

Easter

- During an Easter egg hunt, it is not polite to take an Easter egg from a little kid during the hunt. It's nice to help little kids find some of the eggs.

May Day

- May Day is a worldwide celebration. Some people celebrate by making baskets of treats and leaving them on your doorstep. They may ring the doorbell and run away.

Fourth of July

- If you are going to a fireworks display, it is a good idea to bring some kind of earplugs in case the noise bothers you.

- During a parade, people riding on floats sometimes throw things to the crowd like candy, balls, water bottles, etc. If someone on the float hits you with one of these items, it is an accident.

- Many families will have a picnic outside on the 4th of July. If you don't like eating outside, try to talk to you parents ahead of time to come up with an alternative plan.

- During the 4th of July many people wear clothes that are red, white, and blue. This is a way to honor the colors of the American flag.

Labor Day

- Labor Day is a celebration of working men and women in the United States. Most schools are closed on Labor Day since it is an official holiday.

Halloween

- On Halloween, many children dress up in costumes and go door-to-door collecting candy. If you do this, remember to say "Thank you" and to have your parents or an adult check through your candy before you eat any of it.

- On Halloween, if kids ring your doorbell, instead of telling them to hurry up or to stop bothering you, it's best to say hi and offer candy.

- Costumes on Halloween can be creative and homemade. If you tell someone that their costume is stupid, it would hurt their feelings.

Hidden Curriculum Items: Holidays (cont.)

Thanksgiving

- If you are at Thanksgiving dinner and your uncle's homemade dressing tastes bad, don't tell him, as it would probably hurt his feelings.

- You may hear adults refer to "Black Friday." This is not something bad; it is a day when the traditional Winter season sales begin and stores often have extreme sales to attract shoppers, which is typically the day after Thanksgiving.

- If members of your family gather together to celebrate Thanksgiving, they usually cook a big meal. If you don't like some of the food, refrain from telling your family. This may hurt their feelings.

December Holidays

- Some children believe in Santa Claus bringing gifts on Christmas. If you don't, don't ruin the fun for them, especially young children, by telling them there is no Santa.

- During the holiday season, it's important to remember that not all kids receive the same amount of gifts as you might. If someone asks you what you received during the holidays, it's best to mention one or two gifts, not all of the gifts you received.

Hidden Curriculum Items: Home Life

- Your parents' friends might seem nicer than your parents and may let you do things that your mom or dad wouldn't because they are trying to be nice. Repeatedly saying things like "Why can't my mom be nice" or "Can you teach my mom how to behave" can sound mean and might hurt your mom's feelings.

- In your home, some things belong to you or some other family member, whereas other things belong to the entire family. Ask permission before using something that belongs to other members of the family even if they are not using it at the time.

- Sometimes arguing with your parents, even if you know you are in the right, gets you into more trouble than if you said nothing.

- If you see that something needs to be cleaned up at home, don't wait for your parents to tell you to do it. They will appreciate you helping out all by yourself.

- Don't repeat to others conversations you overhear your parents having about private family matters.

- At family gatherings, if the noise and all the people get to be too much for you, ask an adult if you can go to a different part of the house, where it is quieter.

- When you go out with friends, your parents will probably ask where you are going and whom you are with. They are not being nosy; they care about you and your safety.

- If your parents are working on something or are having a serious discussion, it is best to do something quietly by yourself and wait for them to be available.

- Never tell anyone but your parents your passwords. Don't allow anyone to access your email or computer accounts using your password.

- When you enter a room and someone is watching TV, ask before changing the channel. If the person is not finished watching, you can either join in or ask when the show is over and return at that time to watch your program.

- When you approach a person in a room in your house, make sure she can see or hear you coming so you don't startle her.

- If your parent is tired or not feeling well, it is probably not a good time to ask her to play or to do something really noisy. Try to find a quiet activity.

- When you ask your parents why you have to do something, they sometimes say, "Because I said so." This means that they are not going to discuss the matter with you and that you should not ask them again.

- When there are guests at your house, make sure to put on clothes when you come out of the shower. It is not polite to walk around naked or in just a towel.

- When your parents are lecturing your sister or brother about something they have done wrong, it is not a good idea to laugh or make fun. You may end up getting in trouble yourself.

- If your brother or sister's bedroom door is closed, knock and ask if you can enter before opening the door.

Hidden Curriculum Items: Life Activities

Award Ceremonies

- When at a small formal ceremony where someone is being recognized, don't yell and scream unless everyone else does. Look to see what the audience does and follow along – like looking towards the person, listening quietly.

- If someone is getting an award that you feel you should have received, be polite and congratulate the person anyway.

Camping

- Camping is a fun activity for families to do in the summertime. If you go camping, you may need to use a bathroom that is for everyone on the campsite. It's not O.K. to use someone else's bathroom in their camper unless you have permission.

- When you go camping or hiking, be sure to carry all your trash out of the park with you.

- If you are eating a snack while taking a walk, don't drop your trash on the ground. Put it in your pocket or keep it in your hand until you can put it in a trashcan.

- If you are going to be camping or outdoors in the summer, make sure to take an insect repellant with you. It may smell bad when you spray it on. It's better to use the insect repellant than come home with mosquito bites.

Concerts

- At a piano concert, school play, or similar event, try not to say, "Is this ever going to end?" or "She doesn't play very well!" Or anything else that the performer may find offensive.

- If you see a microphone on a stage, don't run up and try to speak into it. If you want to try out the microphone, ask for permission first.

- If your family goes to a music performance that has tickets, they will typically have reserved seats. It's O.K. if you sit in a different seat than your ticket says as long as it is one of your family's seats.

- If you are attending a performance and the pitch of the music is hurting your ears, quietly ask your parents if you can wait outside the room. It's good to carry earplugs to use in case leaving the room is not an option.

- If the audience really likes a performance, they may stand and clap at the end. This is called a standing ovation. Watch others around you to see whether you should stand.

- When you are at a performance or show, turn off your cell phone and video games. The noise of the ringer and the light from the screen can be distracting to others in attendance as well as the performers.

Department Stores

- Pretending or acting out scenes from a movie in a store can be confusing to those around you. They might not understand what you are doing.

Hidden Curriculum Items: Life Activities (cont.)

Department Stores (cont.)

• If you are out shopping with your family and suddenly are lost, look around to see if there is an adult to help you. Otherwise, stay put to give your family an opportunity to find you.

• When you are checking out of a store, if the employee asks for help from a manager or another co-worker, it doesn't mean that he or she needs to be fired.

• In a department store, it is O.K. to cut in line to ask one question when other people are making purchases. Wait to the side by the cashier and ask your question when the cashier is ringing up the customer or waiting for the customer to pay. Don't interrupt a conversation.

• When trying on shoes in a store, wear socks or borrow some from the store employees.

Elevators

• When you get on an elevator, always stand facing the doors; don't face the back or sides of the elevator, or stare at others.

• When getting off an elevator you are standing besides the panel with the floor numbers, it's polite to use the "open elevator" button and hold the elevator open for other people to get out.

• If you are riding an elevator with a young child, the child might want to have a turn pushing the buttons. Telling her "don't even think about pushing that button" might upset the child or her parents – or both.

Gatherings

• When you are in public, especially at social functions, it is not a good idea to swear or tell rude jokes.

• When you attend a party at a friend's house, make sure you have a ride home when the party is scheduled to be over so you don't inconvenience the host by hanging around afterwards waiting for somebody to pick you up.

• If you are invited to a party and the invitation says RSVP, you are supposed to let the host know whether you will or will not be attending the party.

• When you are having your picture taken, try to look at the camera and smile as if someone said something funny.

• If you are going to a party and the host says to bring a "white elephant" gift, she means something of little value, maybe something you have around your house or something funny.

Listening to Music

• If you are listening to an electronic device with headphones and someone talks to you, remove the headphones so you can hear the other person as well as your own voice volume.

• When around other people, don't sing out loud when listening to music on your headphones. Although you may not hear yourself singing, others will.

Hidden Curriculum Items: Life Activities (cont.)

Listening to Music (cont.)

- People have different tastes in music. It's O.K. that you have different tastes; not everyone will like the same things.

- Even if you like dancing when you are listening to your IPod, most public places are not the appropriate place for it.

Lost and Found

- When you lose something in a store and cannot find it, ask for the lost and found department, which is usually in the customer service area of the store.

- Even if you like an item that you find, it is not yours to keep. It should be returned to the original owner.

- If you find something that someone might have lost in a store, take it to the lost and found department.

- If you see someone drop something, the best thing to do is to say, "Excuse me" to get the person's attention and then say, "Did you drop this (name the item)?"

Money

- It is not polite to ask adults how much money they make.

- If you are out in public and have money, keep it in your pocket. Don't show it to others, especially not to strangers. Never talk or brag about how much money you have with you.

- It is important to learn how to calculate and receive correct change from a clerk in a store.

- If you are short-changed in a restaurant or store, calmly tell the waiter or clerk that you did not receive the correct change before putting the money away or leaving. Tell them what type of money you gave them (e.g., two dimes and one nickel, two ones) and how much change you were expecting. In most cases, the short-changing is an accident.

- When someone standing in the street asks you for money, you don't have to give him money. You don't have to tell him how much money you have. The person may look like she needs money; you still don't have to give any. If you want to give money, don't give away all of your money. You could say, "I don't have any to give" or "This is all I can give you." (This does not apply to muggings. In a mugging, a criminal wants your money or possessions. It is best to give all of your money to a mugger to avoid getting hurt.)

Parks and Playgrounds

- If you are drinking from a public water fountain, keep your mouth off of the spout to prevent sharing germs.

- Public parks and playgrounds can be crowded, so sometimes you may have to wait your turn to use the equipment. You can wait in line or go to another area where there are fewer people.

The Hidden Curriculum

Hidden Curriculum Items: Life Activities (cont.)

Personal Issues

- If you need to pass gas in public, politely go to the restroom. Even in the restroom, it is a good idea to try to pass the gas as quietly as possible.
- If you have an itch in a private area, don't scratch it in public. Go to the restroom or somewhere private.
- If you put on too much cologne or after-shave lotion, it may smell too strong and offend others. Ask someone in your family or a close friend to show you how much to put on at a time.
- It's not considered polite to comb your hair, cut your fingernails, or perform other kinds of personal grooming at the dinner table.
- Be sure to shower or bathe every day, and keep your hair and teeth brushed and your hands and fingernails clean.
- Passing gas in public is not polite. If you accidentally pass gas and others around you notice, just quietly say, "Excuse me."
- Don't talk about how mucus looks or feels in the throat or looks in your tissue.
- Blow your nose discreetly rather than standing in the middle of a room and making a scene.
- Don't sneeze in your hand and then shake hands. Wash your hands first.
- Attend to your personal appearance (runny nose, wet clothes, etc.).

Pranks

- It is not a prank if someone gets hurt. If you hurt someone, it is meanness.
- Some people do pranks on April Fool's Day. They are almost always meant to be funny.
- If something is against the law, it is not a prank. Damaging something usually falls in the category of "against the law."

Public Library

- If you see someone carrying an armload of books, offer to help or to hold the door open.
- When you check out a book from the library, it is important to remember that you are only borrowing it. Take good care of it, don't mark it up or write in it, and return it by the date it is due.

Hidden Curriculum Items: Life Activities (cont.)

Public Transportation

- Sometimes you may have to share a seat with someone when you are riding on a bus. If you have never met the person before, it is O.K. to just sit quietly without talking until you arrive at your bus stop and get off the bus.

- Some modes of public transportation require exact change. Ask a trusted friend or adult if you do not know if exact change is needed. If you need exact change, make sure that you have enough for a round trip. It is polite to let older people sit when limited space is available.

- Know where you need to get off of a bus or subway before you get on. It is also wise to know the schedule of stops.

Stealing

- If kids ask you to steal something from a store (or another person), they are not your friends and you should not do it. Instead, tell an adult you trust.

- Even if you really want something in a store, make sure you have enough money to pay for it. You should never just take it. That is stealing, and that's against the law.

Talking on the Telephone

- When ending a conversation on the phone, make sure the other person has finished what he or she is saying. Then say "Goodbye" and hang up.

- Don't walk up and start talking to someone who is talking on the telephone.

- When taking a phone message, especially from a business, it is important to write down the name, number, time of call, and what the person wants. It is O.K. to ask the caller to repeat what he or she said or to talk a little slower.

- When you answer the phone, say "hello" and before you hang up say "goodbye."

- Don't call people on the phone early in the morning or late at night.

- It is not O.K. to make prank phone calls.

Hidden Curriculum Items: Medical Appointments

- If you are in a waiting room, speak in a very low voice when talking.

- When you visit the doctor, you may have to wait while she is caring for other patients. There may be magazines or a TV in the waiting room to help you pass the time, but bringing something you enjoy doing quietly is always a good idea.

- Sometimes appointments for your parents or other family members take a while. Bring a book or other items to pass the time.

- While in the doctor's waiting room, don't tell others in detail why you are there.

- When you are sitting in the waiting room at a doctor's office, it is not appropriate to ask the other patients what is wrong with them

- Doctors can't fix everything that bothers you. When you visit the doctor, try not to repeatedly ask her to fix things that aren't health related, such as other people bothering you, your brother talking too loudly, your mom not letting you play your video games, etc.

- When you are sitting in the dental chair waiting for the dentist, don't touch the equipment unless the dental assistant or dentist gives you permission.

- Dentists often give out toothbrushes, floss, and toothpaste to their patients. This is a gift to encourage their patients to continue taking care of their teeth.

- Sometimes doctors' offices have a bowl of candy at the counter. If it is out in the waiting area, it is for all the people who are waiting for their appointments.

- If you are visiting someone in the hospital, don't walk down the hallways and look into the rooms of the other patients.

Hidden Curriculum Items: Movie Theatres

- If you invite a friend to a movie, it is polite to offer to pay for them if your parents say that's O.K.

- When you are at the movies and something happens that you don't like, it's very distracting to others if you shout things like "boo, hiss", etc. Its best to sit quietly and hope the movie gets better.

- If you are watching a movie you have seen before with someone who has not seen it, don't refer to events that haven't happened yet. That could spoil the story for your friend.

- Always open your candy or pop before the movie starts. The noise of opening up your candy may bother other people in the movie theatre.

- Whisper when inside a movie theatre.

- When other seats are available in the theatre, leave a space between yourself and a stranger.

- Don't say "fire" in a movie theatre.

- Clap after a play, not a movie.

- It is a good general rule not to do in real life what people do on television or in the movies.

Hidden Curriculum Items: Neighbors

- When you walk past somebody's house, it is not polite to stop and stare through the windows. It could get you in trouble.
- Even if you know someone, don't go into his or her house unless you're invited – not even if the door is open.
- If you notice the neighbor's newspaper lying in their driveway, it is unacceptable to pick it up and take it home. That is stealing.
- If your neighbor's garage door is open, don't walk in and look around unless you are invited. Your neighbors could report you to the police for trespassing.
- When you see a sign that states "Garage Sale" or "Yard Sale" with an address, it does not mean that the people are selling their garage or yard. They are selling items that they don't want or need any more.

Hidden Curriculum Items: Pets

- If you have a pet, it is important that you care for its daily needs (food, water, exercise, grooming). Animals are dependent on their owners to satisfy their needs.
- Never go up and pet a dog you don't know. Always ask the owner if the dog is friendly and likes to be petted. If there is no owner around, stay away from the dog.
- If you meet a person with a service dog, ask if you can pet the dog. It may be busy helping the person, so you need to let it do its job. It performs an important function.
- It's O.K. to be sad about a pet dying. Your friend may have a pet that died. It's nice to say that you are sorry about their loss.
- When your class has a new pet, your teacher may ask for suggestions for a name. Typically, the name chosen is the one that has the most votes. The name you like might not be the one your classmates vote for. It's O.K. if your pet name is not selected.
- Sometimes pets may be in a kennel while their owner is gone or busy. It's best to leave the animal in the kennel instead of letting it out.
- Little dogs may nip at people that attempt to pet them. It is not O.K. to kick the dog if this happens. It's best to walk away and try to remember not to pet that dog again.
- When you visit a friend's house, the family pets may be inside the house. You should try to follow their rules about playing with their pet and not throw toys to try to get their pet to play.
- If you want to talk with other people about your pet, only share two or three things and then ask if they have a pet. People will appreciate your interest in them.

Hidden Curriculum Items: Religious Services and Funerals

- In a place of worship, don't ask loudly when the speaker will be finished. Instead, bring something you can quietly do to help pass the time, if appropriate.

- During worship, when someone comes in late, it's best not to comment on his or her tardiness.

- While out in the community, you may see your priest, pastor, or other clergy outside of church. When you do, it's best to just say "Hi" and not list all the sins in public you think you have committed.

- If someone has different beliefs than you (political, religious, etc.), it is usually best to "agree to disagree." That is, you accept that you believe differently and respect each other for it. You don't have to accept what the other person believes, but be respectful.

- In some places of worship, a plate or basket is passed during the service to collect money as an offering. It is not polite to comment on what others have given, nor is it acceptable to take any money from the offerings.

- When attending a funeral, some people may be very upset and crying. Try not to stare at them or ask them why they are crying.

- Whisper or use a low-volume voice in worship services or at funerals.

- Don't shout hello to your friend two pews ahead of you during religious services.

- During a funeral service, don't laugh out loud or make jokes about the person who died or anything else.

- Wear conservative clothing when going to a house of worship.

The Hidden Curriculum

Hidden Curriculum Items: School

Assignments and Homework

- It is O.K. if you are not the first to finish a classroom assignment or test. Unless the teacher tells you otherwise, speed is not important. But accuracy is.

- If you have a big project due at school, it is a good idea to plan ahead for what you need. It can be difficult to get everything done last minute, and you might forget something important.

- If somebody congratulates you on getting a good grade on a paper, say "Thanks." Don't say you deserved it because you are smarter than anybody else in the class – even if that is true.

- If you allow another student to copy your answers, your teacher may give you an "F" even though your answers were correct. It is not O.K. to cheat.

- When the teacher gives you time at the end of class to start your homework, he does not mean for you to do something else, like look at a magazine you brought from home or draw pictures.

- If you are unable to complete your work at school, take it home to finish it.

- When the teacher says, "do your best," that means you should try your hardest. It does not mean that you will automatically get 100% on the assignment.

- Even though your assignment is complete, you will probably get more points for making your work as neat as possible.

- During class, learn when the teacher will allow you to work on your assignments. You can find this out by asking the teacher.

- If you think that the teacher made a mistake in grading your paper, politely ask if you can talk with him about it.

- If you finish an assignment before other students in the class, work quietly at your desk until the teacher says to stop.

- It is inappropriate to comment on other students' work quality, unless the entire class is discussing how they can improve their work.

- Find out the teacher's rules if you perform poorly on a test or project. Don't have a tantrum or meltdown. Doing poorly on a test usually means that you have to learn to study in a different way. Talk with your parents and teachers so they can help you.

- If I don't want to do an assignment, you can think that quietly inside your head. You still have to do it. If you say something out loud, you may get in trouble.

- If you have a book report to do and reading the entire book feels overwhelming, one option is to go to a bookstore and buy a condensed or abbreviated version to read. Then read the whole book. The reading will go much faster because you will know the plot.

- If you are not sure where to turn in your assignments, watch what other kids do or ask the teacher.

Hidden Curriculum Items: School (cont.)

Bathroom Issues

- Wait until you have shut the bathroom door before you take off any clothing.
- After you use the restroom, always wash your hands.
- Remember to pull up and zip or fasten your pants before you come out of the bathroom.
- Ask permission or get a pass before leaving the classroom to use the bathroom.
- Quietly tell the teacher or an adult you need to use the restroom instead of announcing it to the whole class.
- Don't announce or discuss bathroom issues upon returning to class.
- Avoid yelling to another student that he forgot to zip his zipper. Tell the person quietly.
- If you need special bathroom supplies, you can usually get them from the school nurse.

Behavior in School

- If a kid at school accuses you of doing something wrong that you didn't do, he may be bullying you. It is best not to answer such accusations and find an adult as soon as you can to report the incident.
- When walking in the hallway, singing a song aloud is inappropriate.
- If someone says something mean to you, don't hit or yell at the person. It is best to stay calm and seek help from an adult, if necessary.
- If you are feeling upset, it is best to either talk calmly with a trusted adult or to take a little time to calm down. Yelling or hitting can be misunderstood by others around you and can get you into trouble.
- If another kid in class tells you, "Get out of my face!" he wants you to stop bothering him and to leave him alone.
- If a teacher tells another student to stop talking; it is a good idea for you to also stop talking since the teacher has already expressed disapproval of talking.
- If you get in trouble once, it does not mean that your entire day is ruined.
- When someone else is getting in trouble, it is not the time to ask questions or show the teacher something.
- If the teacher crosses her arm and clears her throat, it means that she either wants the class to be quiet or to look up and get ready to listen to a direction.
- If your teacher gives you a warning about your behavior and you continue the behavior, you will probably get in trouble. If you stop the behavior immediately after the warning, you will probably not get into trouble.

Hidden Curriculum Items: School (cont.)

Bullying/Tattling

- A real friend will not pressure you to take the blame for something he did.

- You don't have to give people money just because they ask you to. If a student at school tells you to give him money, let an adult know, because that is bullying.

- Learn when it is O.K. to tattle. Generally, if someone says, does something, or threatens to do something to hurt someone else or you or property, tell a trusted adult.

- If other students are teasing you, don't get mad and hit them. Tell an adult who can help you.

- If other students are fighting or bullying others, tell the teacher. If they are goofing around in a friendly manner or having pretend fights, don't tell the teacher.

- Don't tattle on what every student is doing wrong. It is up to the teacher to catch the students and reprimand them.

- If one of your classmates tells you to do something you think might get you in trouble, stop and think before acting. Friends don't ask other friends to do things that will get them in trouble.

- Don't pick on other students.

- If someone picks on you or another student, tell the teacher.

Classroom Rules

- If you run out of paper or your pencil breaks while you are taking notes or doing an assignment in class, you are still responsible for finishing the work. Ask someone nearby if you can borrow the supplies you need. Then return the supplies when you are done and say, "Thank you."

- If your class is told to critique each other's work, that means you are to give ideas for how to improve. The comments are not meant to be hurtful or to be taken as a personal attack.

- Before you leave one class to go to another, leave your workspace neat for the next person coming into the class.

- If you know that your teacher has candy in her desk, it's best to leave it alone. If you want a piece, ask your teacher for permission first.

- If your teacher is still talking when the bell rings to change class, wait until she has finished talking before you get up to leave.

- ALWAYS report to the school office or a trusted teacher any conversations you hear about weapons being brought to school.

- Don't talk about guns or knives at school.

- If a teacher or another adult tells a student not to call out in class, for example, it is a good idea to follow the same instructions even if your name was not mentioned.

Hidden Curriculum Items: School (cont.)

Classroom Rules (cont.)

- If you have found something at school that does not belong to you, take it to the Lost and Found or give it to a teacher. Even if you like the item, you cannot just keep it.

- Adjust your voice level according to where you are. It is O.K. to be loud outside, but you should use a quieter voice inside, especially in the classroom.

- If you are late for class, don't argue with the teacher if he disciplines you. Wait until class is over and ask if you can explain why you were late. He may or may not accept your reason.

- Often teachers will ask you to give someone else a message. Instead of yelling it across the room, find the person and give them a message in a calm manner.

- Asking a question when you don't understand something shows the teacher you are paying attention and trying to follow directions. Asking too many questions can be seen as annoying, however.

- Place the cap back on any pen or marker that you have been using.

- Use your own supplies. If you have to borrow something, remember to ask. Never grab or take something without asking first.

- Raise your hand to get the teacher's attention.

- Raise your hand when the teacher pauses, instead of when he is in the middle of explaining something.

- It's O.K. to make a mistake – whiteout or an eraser can be used.

- If someone is doing something in class that is bothering you or making you uncomfortable, ask them to please stop and explain why it bothers you. If they continue, tell an adult.

- Always keep your hands and feet to yourself.

- Be willing to try new activities and skills.

- When saying the Pledge of Allegiance or singing the Star Spangled Banner, refrain from talking or laughing. To help keep your attention on the flag, choose a star on the flag and stare at it while you are saying the pledge or singing.

- Walk inside the classroom; run outside on the playground if you feel like it.

- While working, look at your own paper or book.

- During silent reading, read in your mind, not out loud.

- Be on time to class.

- Make eye contact with the teacher to let him know you are listening. If you can't look him in the eye, look towards his face.

- During the school day you are only allowed to be in certain places of the school. Know which areas are accessible to students.

Hidden Curriculum Items: School (cont.)

- Don't draw violent scenes when drawing or coloring in school.
- In middle and high school, teachers often have different rules. It is important to know the rules for each teacher. If you don't agree with the rules, it will do you no good to say that they are not fair.
- When the teacher is giving a lesson, it is time to listen. You can talk about topics that you are interested in at a later time.
- If you have guest speakers in class, don't interrupt their speech by talking or asking questions. Ask questions at the end of the speech.
- Most teachers don't allow students to chew gum in school. Chew gum after school.
- You will probably be teased if someone sees you tasting glue at school.
- Keep personal information about your family to yourself during school.
- Even if other students write in their textbooks or on their desks, use a piece of paper instead so you won't get in trouble.
- When it is time to clean up, it does not have to be perfect. The janitor will come in after school to vacuum and do the final cleanup.
- When standing in line, make sure there is enough space for one or two people between you and the person in front of you.

Fire Drills

- It's a rule that schools have fire drills throughout the school year. Even though you've already practiced it once, you will need to participate each time there is a drill.
- Never yell "Fire!" or pull a fire alarm unless there really is a fire. It is not only dangerous but also against the law, so you could get into big trouble.
- Schools have fire drills and other emergency practice procedures so everyone will know what to do in case of a real emergency. Take such practices seriously and follow your teacher's directions.
- During a fire drill, go with your class to the nearest exit and get outside. This is not the time to go to the bathroom or even ask to go to the bathroom.
- Remember to be quiet. This is not the time to talk or ask questions.
- It is O.K. to cover your ears to drown out the sound of the alarm when you are exiting the building.

Hidden Curriculum Items: School (cont.)

Extracurricular Activities

- If you are in a play at school and someone tells you to "Break a leg!" he is not really hoping you will get hurt. It is a phrase that means, "Good luck and do well!!"

- When you are cheering for your school's team, it is best to yell encouragement to the team in general and not to say negative things about the opposing team.

- Many schools have "Spirit Weeks" where people dress up in different themes each day. On those days it is O.K. to wear clothing you wouldn't normally wear to school, such as PJs on Pajama Day.

- In choir class, some student may not be on tune or have a good voice. It's not polite to say that one of your classmates is an awful singer. It's best to try to not say anything.

- When your school band is rehearsing, it will hurt the teacher's feelings if you say that the band doesn't sound good.

- The first year in band class, not all students have a brand new instrument. It's O.K. to use a pre-owned instrument. They work just as good as brand new instruments.

- After a music concert or drama performance, it is common for teachers to have their students watch the concert or performance on tape. You may not want to watch the concert or performance, but it's good to watch it from the audience perspective.

- If you are in strings class, it's not wise to use the bows as swords. Bows can be extremely expensive and you can hurt someone by accidently hitting them with the bow.

Group Projects

- When working on a group project, be open to others' suggestions and ideas even if you don't like them at first.

- When you are assigned to a group, stay with that group until the teacher changes the arrangement.

- During group assignments in class, everybody in the group is responsible for doing the work.

Library

- Use a whisper or low-volume voice in the library.

- Check out the books that you are interested in before taking them out of the library.

- If the book you want to check out is not in, see the librarian about placing it on reserve for you.

- Try not to stand over someone's shoulder when they are checking email.

Hidden Curriculum Items: School (cont.)

Getting Along With Classmates

- It is not your role in school to tell the other students what they can and what they cannot do. Leave that up to the adults.

- If you overhear classmates planning a get-together, it is not appropriate to invite yourself along. You should wait to be asked.

- If you are whispering with another student and suddenly stop when someone else walks into the room, the person approaching you may think you are talking about him and be offended.

- If you are having a party and don't plan to invite everyone in your class, don't pass out the invitations during class. The students who are not invited might feel bad.

- If you pass notes in class to a friend, do it discreetly so the teacher does not catch you. Passing notes can get you in trouble. If you don't want to get in trouble, don't pass notes.

- When saying goodbye before summer break, classmates may say, "See you next year!" They are not talking about the following January, just the start of the new school year in August or September.

Locker Room Rules

- It is appropriate to fix your hair and look at yourself in the mirror before and after P.E.

- If there are people taking showers or changing their clothes, don't stare at them or make comments about their bodies.

- Change into your P.E. clothes in the locker room, not the hallway.

- It is not appropriate to use other people's locker items without asking and receiving permission first, even if they are your friend.

- When you are taking a shower in a group setting, it is not appropriate to sustain eye contact or watch others take showers.

- It is not appropriate to touch others in the restroom or shower.

- Follow what the crowd does to know when it is appropriate to shower.

- Learn where to change clothes and if total nudity is appropriate.

Hidden Curriculum Items: School (cont.)

Lockers and the Hallway

- Don't leave valuables in your school locker or in the gym locker room. If you bring an electronic device, keep it in your pocket or in some other out-of-sight place.

- Try to carry enough pencils and paper for school or store them in your locker. It is O.K. to borrow from another student or the teacher if you forget, but you should not do that every day.

- If someone is in your way when you are walking down the hallway at school, politely say, "Excuse me" and allow the person time to move out of your way before you go on.

- When you are walking in the hallway or on the stairs at school or other places, as much as possible, stay to the right so people going the other direction can pass without bumping into you.

- Turn the dial on your combination lock after you close your locker. This prevents others from opening your locker easily.

- When walking up and down stairs, stay on the right side and try not to crowd the person in front of you.

- If you have older or younger siblings at school, don't yell and be angry with them when they are with their friends. It will embarrass them.

- Don't let people (friends, strangers or adults) store backpacks or other bags in your locker without seeing what is inside. Ask permission before looking in their backpacks or bags.

- Sometimes boys and girls will be standing by a locker, hugging and/or kissing. It is best to ignore them instead of making a comment or staring.

Lunchroom

- When you are eating with others during lunch or snack time, it is a good idea to take small bites and chew with your mouth closed.

- In the lunchroom, a table may be designated for students with peanut allergies. Make sure to check your lunch for peanut products before sitting at that table.

- When you choose something for lunch from the cafeteria, once you have touched it, don't put it back. Others don't want to eat food that you have touched.

- Even if someone has extra food on his plate, you cannot help yourself to it without permission.

- Parents sometimes pack their children lunch instead of having them eat the food in the cafeteria. If your friend has something that you don't like, try to ignore it and not say anything about it.

- In the lunchroom, begin eating right away so you don't waste time.

- Talk in a low-volume voice in the lunchroom.

- Don't yell across the lunchroom to your friends.

- Avoid bringing tuna fish in your lunch. It smells, and kids sometimes won't want to sit by you.

- Never throw food in the lunchroom, even if other students do.

Hidden Curriculum Items: School (cont.)

Nurse's Office

- Don't bring any kind of medicine to school unless you have a doctor's note. If so, take it directly to the school health office.
- NEVER share medicines with other kids at school.

Recess and P.E.

- During P.E. class, you may get a ball that is a different color than your friends. The teacher is not concerned about the color, but the type of ball you are using.
- Even though the weather is nice outside, you might have indoor recess if it rained because it is too muddy to play outside.
- When lightning is coming close to a school, most schools will have students on the playground come inside for safety reasons. Sometimes it doesn't look like lightning is close, but teachers and your principal have to make sure that everyone is safe.
- If your teacher tells you that you are "on the right track," he means that you are headed towards the right conclusion.
- If your team loses at a game in P.E., don't blame those who did not play well. Try to encourage your teammates to do better next time instead.
- When playing a game, usually someone wins and someone loses. It is O.K. to lose. After it is over, it is polite to tell the other person, "Good game."
- Learn the rules of the games played at recess or P.E. If necessary, ask the recess teacher or P.E. teacher to explain.
- If you are throwing a ball to someone in the gym or at recess, say her name out loud and wait until she looks and has her hands out before throwing it.
- When playing tag, touch the other person softly as if you were petting a dog.
- If you lose a game at recess, it is O.K. Usually the reason you play the game is to learn new skills or enjoy time with other people, not to win all the time.
- On the playground, students must share the equipment.
- When playing a game with teams, realize that everyone likes to have a turn.
- Encourage your teammates by saying positive, polite words, giving "high fives," and staying on the same team.
- During hide-and-seek, count to 10 while your eyes are closed before starting to look.
- When the whistle blows, it is usually time to line up from recess.
- It is O.K. to be loud on the playground. When it is time to go back inside, it is time to be quiet.

Hidden Curriculum Items: School (cont.)

Rules When Talking to the Teacher

- When the teacher is disciplining the entire class, it is not a good time to explain why you think you are not at fault.

- Students may come up with nicknames for the teachers at your school. Always address the teacher by the name she tells you to call her, not one of the nicknames you hear.

- It is O.K. not to like all of your teachers. But you still have to respect them and be polite.

- If you are in a noisy place, like the gym at school, it is O.K. to cover your ears to block some of the noise. But if a teacher or other adult comes up to talk to you, remove your hands from your ears and listen to what they say.

- If you think that the teacher made a mistake, it is not appropriate to correct her in front of everyone. Wait until after class and approach her privately to discuss it.

- If the teacher is talking on the telephone or to an adult, he is probably having a private conversation and you should not listen in.

- Even if you are sitting in the back of the classroom, it is not O.K. to talk while the teacher is talking. It is disrespectful. Besides, the teacher will most likely notice you talking, which can get you in trouble.

- If you disagree with what a teacher is saying, politely say what you think and wait for an answer. If you still disagree, let it go.

- Use a pleasant voice when talking to teachers. They will respond to you in a more positive way.

- Talk to your teacher in a different way than you talk to your friends. Always use a polite voice when speaking to your teacher.

- Refrain from saying rude comments to teachers like "You are old" or "You look really tired today."

- Teachers don't know all of the answers. It is O.K. if they have to look something up or ask someone else.

- Teachers use nonverbal communication to send messages to students. Sometimes teachers look at students, stand close to them, or raise or lower their voice to get their message across. If you don't understand what the teacher is trying to communicate, ask her politely to explain.

- After a teacher returns from maternity leave, tell her congratulations. Don't tell her that she is still fat even if she may look that way.

- If you talk to the principal, avoid telling her that if she listened better, more kids would like her.

- Never call your teacher a bad name to her face or when other adults are around.

Hidden Curriculum Items: School (cont.)

School Bus

- When you ride a bus to and from school, the bus drivers may have to practice an emergency evacuation off the bus. Remember to remain calm, quiet and listen for directions. Learning how to evacuate the bus is important to know in an emergency.

- When a school bus comes across railroad tracks, the bus may stop and open the door to listen for a train. Just because the driver opens the door, it doesn't mean that it's time to get off the bus.

- When riding on the bus, you might not always get to sit in your favorite spot.

- When the bus stops at a railroad track and the driver tells the kids to "be quiet" she doesn't mean you can whisper, she actually means "be silent" (NO talking) so she can listen for any trains.

Substitute Teachers

- If you have a substitute teacher, he may or may not enforce the same rules as your regular teacher. While he is acting as your teacher, you will need to follow his rules.

- Substitutes will often turn the lights off if the classroom is too noisy. If you notice the teacher turning off the lights, it's best to stop talking.

Transitions

- Having a schedule is a good thing, but sometimes schedules change. Change is not bad. If you have a question about a change in schedule, ask an adult who knows what's going on.

- If there is a change at school and you feel upset, you can take deep breaths and try to stay calm. Yelling out "That's not fair" or "Oh no" is not a good idea. It may upset others.

- Usually at the beginning of a school year, you will be assigned a new teacher. Each teacher may have different classroom rules. It is not your job to tell the teacher that last year's teacher had different rules. You just have to learn the new rules.

- Teachers give students transition statements – learn what your teacher uses so you can be ready to go to the next subject or activity. For example, teachers may tell you that you will be leaving in 5 minutes. That may mean 2 minutes or 10 minutes. You will not know the exact time, but at least you will know that you are leaving soon.

Hidden Curriculum Items: Social Interactions

Basic Rules

- Don't expect every rule to be "fair."

- If someone calls you a name and you are not sure what it means, don't repeat it until you find out. It could be some kind of inappropriate slang that might be offensive to others.

- Older kids usually think that once you are in middle school, it is not cool to hug and kiss your parents around friends. You can hug them when it is just your family at home or if you are leaving for a trip.

- If you are a boy, even though a particular girl band or a girl singer is cool, others will think it is strange if you try to imitate them.

- Never point with your middle finger. It is very impolite and would be offensive to the person who sees it.

- Don't tell others that they have bad breath even if they do.

- Don't make negative comments about anyone's outfit or hairdo.

- Don't yell out, "Someone farted and it stinks!" If you think that someone has passed gas, it is best to just ignore it.

- Don't pick your teeth or other body parts (ears, nose) in class or public areas.

- Don't pick your bottom in class even if it itches or your underwear rides up. Do this in the bathroom.

- Don't pick at scabs or play with them during class.

- When you are with people whom you don't know well, don't pass gas, pick your nose, or scratch a private body part.

- Don't explain to a person with a new puppy that the breed she bought has a terribly aggressive disposition.

- Don't tell a neighbor that her house is much dirtier than it should be.

- Don't cut in line when buying tickets for a movie or a concert.

- Treat others with respect.

- Take responsibility for your actions.

- Wait, wait, wait.

- Breaking the law is never a good idea, no matter what your reason is.

- Seek out an adult if you are hurt or cannot handle a certain situation.

- Control your anger.

- Don't point out "funny bumps" on people's faces or ask them if they have pimples or zits.

- Even if you think someone's hair is pretty, try not to touch it.

Hidden Curriculum Items: Social Interactions (cont.)

Making Conversation

- It's important to respond when someone calls out to you. If you don't answer, the person will think you didn't hear. She might also think you are ignoring her on purpose and get upset.

- If somebody makes a grammatical error while speaking, it is not polite to interrupt and correct him.

- Find out what music is cool. Opera or classical music is usually not cool when you are a teenager. Some kids do like opera or classical music, but they don't talk about it.

- Be careful about HOW you say things; your tone of voice has just as much of an impact – sometimes even more – as the words you use.

- When you are talking with someone, try to look in his direction and use his name. It shows the person that you are paying attention and that you care about him and what he is saying.

- Maintain eye contact while talking with people.

- Say the other person's name to get her attention before starting to speak.

- Discuss other topics besides only those that you are interested in.

- Take turns in conversation.

- Who you are with determines what you should talk about. For example, you can talk about a new CD with a friend. You probably would not do this with an adult.

- Others may not always agree with you or you may not agree with others when talking. That is O.K.

- If you are not interested in what others are talking about, try to disguise your disinterest by smiling, nodding, and asking a question about the topic.

- When making conversation, avoid constantly telling others how good you are at something. This usually makes other kids avoid being around you.

- Even if you are really good at something, don't brag about it. If other people are talking about what they are good at, then you can share your talent.

- Wanting to know the answer to a specific question should not be more important than the feelings of the people around you who might be embarrassed by your question.

- Think about the words you are saying. Are they kind, nice or necessary?

- It is not polite to interrupt others while they are talking.

- You don't have to make a comment about yourself every time someone tells you a story about himself. If you do that, most people see you as a "know it all" and eventually stop telling you stories.

- Keep approximately an arm's distance away from the person you are talking with.

Hidden Curriculum Items: Social Interactions (cont.)

Making Conversation (cont.)

- If someone asks you a personal question, it is O.K. to say that you are uncomfortable answering.

- People usually pause to take a breath once in a while when talking. They may even wait a little bit before talking again. Sometimes, people take a little time to formulate a thought or study your reaction to what they're saying. This pause does not mean that they are done talking. Wait at least 5-10 seconds before talking if you are not sure they are done.

Reading Body Language

- People use a lot of what's called "nonverbal communication." This means that instead of, or in addition to, speaking words, they communicate by using facial expressions or moving body parts, like frowning (they are mad) or shrugging their shoulders (they don't know something). Watch for these movements to help you understand what is being communicated.

- If you want to understand someone's thoughts and feelings, it is best to watch the area around their eyes and not the movement of their mouth.

- If your friend raises his eyebrows and opens his eyes wide while you are talking, he is expressing surprise or excitement about what you are saying.

Relationships

- When you kiss someone, don't have gum in your mouth.

- If you like a boy or a girl, you often pretend that you don't like them at all.

- When two people are standing close and speaking very softly, they are having a private conversation. Generally, don't join the conversation without asking first. If the people are two of your really good friends, you can probably join the conversation. If you are unsure what to do, it is best to ask.

- If a classmate of the opposite sex is nice to you, this does not mean that he/she is your boyfriend/girlfriend. Going around and telling your classmates and friends will make it very difficult to have relationships in the future.

- When you see someone in the hall at school or out in the community that you are attracted to, find a way to let the person know without going directly up and saying loudly, "You're cute!" This is embarrassing to the recipient of the comment.

Social Rules

- Not everyone you meet will be a flexible thinker. Shouting, "Don't be a rock brain" may not help the situation.

- If you overhear someone say something about another person that might hurt that person's feelings, it probably wouldn't be a good thing to tell him. You might talk with a trusted adult instead.

- When someone says, "Excuse me," it generally means that you are in the way and that they want you to move.

Hidden Curriculum Items: Social Interactions (cont.)

Social Rules (cont.)

- It is polite to smile when someone greets you. It makes the other person feel good and sends the message that you are happy to see him.

- When you see someone from a different culture, it's not polite to ask them, "What are you," or "Where are you from?"

- If someone gets too close to you and makes you uncomfortable, you can let them know that you need space by saying, "Please move back; I need some room."

- When you are talking with others, don't just go on and on about how good you are at something. They will get the impression that you only think of yourself and may not want to talk with you.

- If another person makes a comment to you that you think is rude, it is a good idea to not make a rude comment back.

- If you notice that someone's pants are unzipped, tell him quietly or let him know in some way that doesn't bring attention to him, so he won't be embarrassed.

- Don't go up to people and smell them, no matter whether you like or dislike the smell.

- When someone tries to help you, be patient and say "Thank you."

- Always be on time.

- Knock before entering a room, except when entering your classroom or a room in your house (except the bathroom).

- Although it is O.K. to say "hi" to everyone you walk by in a small town, this could get you in trouble in large cities.

- People act differently in different situations. Sometimes people treat you differently when they are around certain people.

- Refrain from making negative comments; try to be as polite as possible.

- When people are crying or are angry, don't laugh, as it will make them feel worse.

- When someone asks "How do you like my new _____ ," they usually really want you to tell them you like it. Even if you don't like it, try to find something positive to say.

- When you leave a situation or place, always say goodbye.

- It is appropriate to shake hands with a stranger; hugging is O.K. if the person is a friend.

- Don't hit other people.

- If someone intrudes into your space, ask him politely to move over without touching him.

Hidden Curriculum Items: Social Interactions (cont.)

Social Rules (cont.)

- While it might be O.K. to cuss in private, it is not appropriate to do so in public, especially when adults are near.
- If you respond with no enthusiasm to someone who is talking with great enthusiasm, she will probably stop talking with you.
- When hearing someone speak using incorrect grammar, don't correct him every time.
- There are certain questions that you don't ask others (weight, age, income, religion) if you have just met them.
- Many words have double meanings, like the word "key," for example. Sometimes "key" means a metal object; at other times it means a plastic credit card like a pass. When someone says to use a key in a hotel room or other place, keep this in mind.
- If you forget the name of someone you just met, say politely, "I'm sorry, I forgot your name." The person will usually respond back with his or her name.
- Sometimes people bend the truth a little if it means sparing someone's feelings. For example, if someone asks you if you like his or her shirt and you don't, it is probably best to say something like, "That shirt is great." Or "I really like the colors in your shirt."
- When you try to find a seat to sit in, make sure that someone else is not planning to sit there. One way to find out is to see if they left something on or near the chair to save the seat for when they return.

Telling Jokes

- Repeating the very same joke after someone else has said it to the class will make others laugh at you, not the joke.
- Jokes that you tell friends are usually different from the jokes that you tell adults.
- Don't tell inappropriate jokes to a group of girls if you are a boy, such as jokes about private parts, etc.
- If you do something funny, it is usually only funny once. If you do it repeatedly, it makes you look silly and goofy.
- You may hear and enjoy "dirty jokes." Dirty jokes are usually about sex. It is best to keep these jokes to yourself. Especially don't tell dirty jokes to the opposite sex. Also, jokes or arguments about religion and politics should be avoided.
- Some people laugh when they are making fun of someone. They are not laughing because they think that person is funny. Don't do this because it is hurtful to the person who is being made fun of.

Hidden Curriculum Items: Social Networking

- Make sure that you know the age restrictions on using social media and do not violate them!

- Only allow friends you know on to your Facebook and Twitter. Keep your personal and contact information private.

- Be careful about putting too much personal information on social networking web pages. Strangers may be able to access that information.

- Never agree to meet someone who has only contacted you on the Internet without your parents' knowledge. There are adults who pretend to be younger in order to meet children and teens and those kinds of people can be dangerous.

- Remember that all of your Facebook and Twitter friends can see what you write.

- It is best not to post anything on Facebook when you are upset, angry, or overwhelmed. If you feel like you need to share your feelings, type them in a document. Read the document after you have calmed down and make whatever changes are needed before you post it. It might be helpful to ask a trusted adult or friend to read what you wrote before you post it.

- A Facebook friend is not necessarily a true friend. They are not likely to act in a way that a true friend does. For example, a Facebook friend may not take the time to help you if you need it.

Hidden Curriculum Items: Sporting Events

- If you are wearing a hat at a sporting event and the national anthem is played, you are supposed to take your hat off and stand up while it is being played.

- If someone gets hurt at a ballgame, it is a sign of support when people clap – not applause.

- At sporting events, it is normal to stand and cheer throughout the game. Don't stand the entire time unless everyone else does.

Hidden Curriculum Items: Swimming Pool

Buying a Swimsuit

- Always wear underwear when you try on a bathing suit at the store before buying it.

- Never buy a white bathing suit because your skin will show through when the suit gets wet.

- Make sure the suit you wear is a suitable style for your body shape and size. Ask others if you are not sure.

At the Swimming Pool

- When you are at a public pool, usually there is a shower available to rinse off under before and after you get into the pool. This helps keep the pool clean.

- Sometimes you may have to wait in line at the pool's diving board or slide. It is good to wait quietly and in line until it's your turn.

- Change into your swimming suit at home or in the bathroom at the pool.

- Always wear sunscreen if you are in the sun. Everyone at the pool may not like using sunscreen – don't force others to wear it.

- Once you are on the deck at the pool, refrain from making loud comments about other people's bodies or bathing suits.

- Not everyone at the pool will be swimming. Some people like to lie out in the sun and tan.

- If someone accidentally splashes water on you, it is O.K.. If you don't like to be splashed, move away from the water or the person splashing.

- If you have to go to the bathroom while you are in the pool, get out of the pool and use the bathroom, not the outside shower or the pool.

- For females, if you are in the middle of your menstrual cycle, don't go into the pool unless you are wearing a tampon. If people ask why you are not swimming, tell them you don't feel like swimming.

- If you are thirsty from swimming, don't drink the pool water. Go to the water fountain or drink from the sink in the dressing room (unless there is a sign saying that the water is not for drinking), or buy some pop or water from the concession stand.

Hidden Curriculum Items: Texting/Cell Phones/Email

- It is rude to text when someone is talking to you. Wait until the conversation is over.

- Don't use all capital letters in an email or text message. The receiver will think you are yelling at her.

- When one of your friends texts or instant messages you, she might use abbreviations like "ttyl" (talk to you later). Be sure to ask what such terms mean if you don't know.

- Before you text a friend, find out if he is allowed to text and how much and when he is allowed to text.

- Check with your parents to see if you have texting service and whether you have unlimited texting or if you have to pay per text. It can be very expensive to go over your limit of texts.

- Many students have cell phones with cameras. It is not O.K. to use your cell camera to take pictures of someone and send them to others' phones without getting the permission of the person in the picture.

- If you receive an email that asks for personal information or invites you to a website you are not familiar with, don't reply but show the email to your parent or an adult you trust.

- When you send someone an email, you cannot take it back once you hit the "send" button, so be very careful about what you write.

- Don't put your email address into advertisers' websites. If you do, you will receive email not only from their sites but also from others, as many companies sell information to other sites.

- If you are sitting next to somebody who is reading email, it is not polite to lean over to try to read what she is writing or reading.

- Remember that anything that you text or email can be forwarded to other people – and you may not know them.

- Do not text or email sensitive or private information, including pictures.

Hidden Curriculum Items: Vacations

- When staying at a hotel, remember not to have the volume of the television up too high. You may disturb people in the next room.

- Going on vacation can bring lots of changes and challenges. Remember it will only be a short time before your schedule returns to normal. While you are on vacation, try to enjoy new places and things to do.

- When your family goes on vacation, each person may want to do different things. Don't insist on doing only what you want to do, but be willing to try what others choose.

- When you are at the pool or the beach, be careful to avoid walking over people who are lying on their towels. It might make them uncomfortable and they might get upset if you drip water or sand on them.

- People sometimes like to build sand castles while at the beach. It is not O.K. to knock someone else's castle down unless they ask you to.

- When you visit the zoo they may not have an animal that you want to see. You may politely ask someone who works at the zoo if they have a particular animal. If they don't have the animal you want to see it's not the zoo worker's fault.

- When you are at the beach it can be fun to play in the sand. Sand sticks to things, including your wet clothes, your beach bag, towel, etc. This is O.K. and just part of going to the beach. When you get home or to the parking lot, you can usually shake the sand out of your things.

Hidden Curriculum Items: Video Games/Arcades

- If you are at an arcade and someone is playing the game you want to play, don't stand right behind him and make comments about hurrying up. Just wait nearby until the person is finished.

- Video and arcade games are considered games of chance. They are designed to get you to keep putting money in them without winning a prize.

- If you enter a room and see that someone is intently playing a video game, just watch. Don't ask questions or tell the person how to play unless you are asked. You might distract the player and mess up his game.

- If you see someone is playing a handheld video game in a public place, it is not polite to just sit down and look over his shoulder. Ask if he would mind you watching and then sit quietly beside him.

- When someone is excited and tells you about his latest score in a game, tell him, "Good job." Then ask about the game rather than saying that you scored higher or that the game was easy.

- If your parents ask you to stop playing a video or computer game, you may ask if you can save where you are or finish the turn, but if they insist, follow their direction and turn off the game.

- When you play video games with a friend, it is a good idea to pick a game that both of you can play at the same time. Another option is to take turns often so no one gets stuck watching the other person play for too long.

- It's O.K. to enjoy playing video or computer games, but you should not do it all the time. It's important to do a variety of activities and get physical exercise as well.

Figurative Speech and Idioms

The following is a small, random sampling of the kinds of idioms and figurative language that cause difficulty for individuals with social-cognitive challenges, who tend to interpret language literally. For additional examples, please go to: http://www.freesearch.co.uk/dictionary.

Term	Meaning
All ears	Listening intently to the speaker
All thumbs	Clumsy
Bent out of shape	Get angry or upset about something not very important
Bite my head off	Speak to someone in a quick, angry way – usually for no good reason
Bite the bullet	Force yourself to do something unpleasant or difficult, or to be brave in a difficult situation
Bite off more than he can chew	Taking on more than he is able to handle
Brainstorming	Suggesting all kinds of ideas to try
Buckle down and get busy	Start working hard
Bull in a china closet	Very careless in the way that they move or behave
Can't make a silk purse out of sow's ear	You can't make something good out of something that is naturally bad
Cat got your tongue	Being quiet and not talking
Coughing their head off	Coughing really hard and very often
Curiosity killed the cat	Said to warn someone not to ask too many questions about something
Cry wolf	Alarming others when there is no real danger
Cut the cheese	Passing gas
Don't be smart	When you speak to other people in a way that shows a lack of respect
Down in the dumps	Unhappy

Figurative Speech and Idioms (cont.)	
Term	**Meaning**
Driving me crazy	Making someone annoyed or angry
Eagle eye	Somebody who sees very well and notices things
Elbow partner	The person sitting next to you
Eyes and knees on me	Sit on the floor looking toward the speaker with your knees pointing toward the speaker, too
Fall back	Refers to when some areas of the country turn their clock back an hour in the autumn
Feeling blue	Sad
Fifty-fifty	Split the cost or item with another person
Fit to be tied	Extremely frustrated/angry
Get it off of your chest	Tell someone about something that has been worrying you or making you feel guilty for a long time
Giving 110%	Doing their best
Get out of my face	A rude way of telling someone that he or she is annoying you and should stop
Go fly a kite	Used to tell someone who is annoying to go away
Golden Rule	Treat others as you want others to treat you
Hat trick	In sports, the same player scoring three goals
Have eyes in the back of your head	Know everything that is happening around you
Heart of gold	Being very kind and generous
Hold your horses	Wait or slow down
Horsing around	Playing or goofing around

Figurative Speech and Idioms (cont.)	
Term	**Meaning**
How the cookie crumbles	Said when something slightly unlucky has happened but it could not have been prevented and so must be accepted
I'm so mad I could split nails	Very angry
In a pig's eye	Something that is highly unlikely
In hot water	To be in or get into a difficult situation in which you are in danger of being criticized or punished
I've got your back	Someone is there to help and support you
Joined at the hip	When two friends always seem to be together.
Knock it off	Used to tell someone to stop doing something that annoys you
Lemon	Something that was bought (e.g. car) that is defective or has problems
Mad as a hornet	Very angry
Mad as a wet hen	Very angry
Make a mountain out of a molehill	Make a slight difficulty seem like a serious problem
Monkey see, monkey do	Copy or imitate someone
Off the top of your head	Name the first idea that occurs to you without giving it much thought
On the ball	Quick to catch on or understand
On the right track	Headed towards the right conclusion
Open mouth, insert foot	Say something by accident that embarrasses or upsets someone, including yourself
Out in left field	No clue/strange
Over the hill	Being too old, especially to do a particular job

Figurative Speech and Idioms (cont.)	
Term	**Meaning**
Pulling my leg	Try to persuade someone to believe something that is not true as a joke
Pulling the wool over my eyes	Deceive someone in order to prevent them from discovering something
Put a lid on it!	Be quiet
Put a sock in it!	Be quiet
Put on your thinking cap	Think seriously about something
Quiet as a mouse	Be very quiet
Quit horsing around	Stop behaving in a silly and noisy way
Roll with the punches	Be able to deal with a series of difficult situations
Running off at the mouth	Talk too much in a loud and uncontrolled way
See red	Become very angry
See ya later, alligator	A farewell paired with, "After a while, crocodile"
Shotgun	The front passenger seat in the car
Sit on your bumper	Sit with your bottom on the floor
Smarty pants	Refers to a person who acts like he knows everything
So hungry I could eat a horse	You are extremely hungry
Spring ahead	When some areas of the country set their clocks ahead by an hour in the spring
Start the ball rolling	Do something that starts an activity, or to start doing something as a way to encourage others to do the same
Straighten up	Behave well after behaving badly
Switch gears	Change subject and move on to something else

Figurative Speech and Idioms (cont.)	
Term	**Meaning**
That cracks me up	Suddenly make someone laugh a lot
Take a chill pill	Relax, not getting upset or excited about something
Tied up in knots	Your stomach is tight and uncomfortable because you are nervous or excited
Top dog	A person who has achieved a position of authority
Think outside the box	Being creative and coming up with new ways of doing something or solving a problem
Under your hat	Keeping whatever was told a secret
Uptight	Worried or nervous and unable to relax
Wait a minute	Wait for a little while, not an exact measurement of time
Watch your p's and q's	Be very careful about how you behave
When donkeys fly	You mean that it will never happen
When it rains, it pours	Said when one bad thing happens, followed by a lot of other bad things, which make a bad situation worse
Winding down	Gradually relax after doing something that has made you tired or worried
You kill me	Amuse someone very much

Slang Terms	
Term(s)	**Context/Definition**
Hey Dog?	How are you?
Hey bro! Hey sis!	A greeting, a sign of friendship
Just chill!	Calm down, relax.
Phat, snap!	Cool.
Shut up!, Get out!, Go on!	You're kidding!, Really? I can't believe it. No way! Get out of here! (Never said to adults.)
Talk to the hand 'cause the face ain't listening!	I don't want to listen to what you are saying.
Way!	Yes.

References

Aspy, R., & Grossman, B. (2011). *Designing comprehensive interventions for high-functioning individuals with autism spectrum disorders: The Ziggurat Model – Release 2.0.* Shawnee Mission, KS: AAPC Publishing.

Barnes, E. (1998). *A little book of manners: Courtesy & kindness for young ladies.* Eugene, OR: Harvest House Publishers.

Barnes, B., & Barnes, E. (2000). *A little book of manners for boys.* Eugene, OR: Harvest House Publishers.

Bieber J. (1994). *Learning disabilities and social skills with Richard LaVoie: Last one picked ... first one picked on.* Washington, DC: Public Broadcasting Service.

Buron, K. D., & Curtis, M. (2012). *The incredible 5-point scale. The significantly improved and expanded second edition.* Shawnee Mission, KS: AAPC Publishing.

Carter, E. W., Austin, D., & Trainor, A. A. (2012). Predictors of postschool employment outcomes for young adults with severe disability. *Journal of Disability Policy Studies, 23,* 50-63.

Centers for Medicare and Medicaid Services. (2010). *Autism spectrum disorders: Final report on environmental scan.* Washington, DC: Author. Retrieved from http://www.impaqint.com/files/4-content/1-6-publications/1-6-2-project-reports/finalasdreport.pdf.

Cornbleth, C. (2011, February 22). *School curriculum: Hidden curriculum.* Retrieved from http://education.stateuniversity.com/pages/1899/Curriculum-School-HIDDEN-CURRICULUM.html.

Debbaudt, D. (2002). *Autism, advocates, and law enforcement professionals: Recognizing and reducing risk situations for people with autism spectrum disorders.* London: Jessica Kingsley.

Endow, J. (2012). *Learning the hidden curriculum: The odyssey of one autistic adult.* Shawnee Mission, KS: AAPC Publishing.

Espeland, P. (2003). *Life lists for teens.* Minneapolis, MN: Free Spirit Publishing, Inc.

Gagnon, E. (2001). *The Power Card strategy: Using special interests to motivate children and youth with Asperger Syndrome.* Shawnee Mission, KS: AAPC Publishing.

Garnett, K. (1984). Some of the problems children encounter in learning a school's hidden curriculum. *Journal of Reading, Writing and Learning Disabilities International, 1*(1), 5-10.

Grandin, T. (1995). *Thinking in pictures and other reports from my life with autism.* New York, NY: Vintage Books.

Hemmings, A. (2000). The hidden curriculum corridor. *High School Journal, 83*(2), 1-10.

Henry, S. A., & Myles, B. S. (2007). *The Comprehensive Autism Planning Systems (CAPS) for individuals with Asperger Syndrome, autism and related disabilities: Integrating best practices throughout the student's day.* Shawnee Mission, KS: AAPC Publishing.

Hudson, J., & Coffin, A. B. (2007). *Out and about: Preparing children with autism spectrum disorders to participate in their communities.* Shawnee Mission, KS: AAPC Publishing.

Jackson, P. (1968). *Life in classrooms.* New York: Holt, Rinehart, & Winston.

Kanpol, B. (1989). Do we dare teach some truths? An argument for teaching more "hidden curriculum." *College Student Journal, 23,* 214-217.

Kauchak, T. (2002). *I can do anything!: Smart cards for strong girls.* Middleton, WI: Pleasant Company Publications.

Koenig, K., De Los Reyes, A., Cicchetti, D., Scahill, L., & Klin, A. (2009). Group intervention to promote social skills in school-age children with pervasive developmental: Reconsidering disorder efficacy. *Journal of Autism and Developmental Disorders, 39,* 1163-1172.

LaVoie, R. (1994). Learning disabilities and social skills with Richard LaVoie. In J. Bieber (Ed.), *Last one picked ... first one picked on.* Washington, DC: Public Broadcasting Service.

Loomis, J. W. (2008). *Staying in the game: Providing social opportunities for children and adolescents with autism spectrum disorders and other developmental disabilities.* Shawnee Mission, KS: AAPC Publishing.

Madden, K. (2002). *Writing smarts: A girl's guide to writing great poetry, stories, school reports, and more!* Middleton, WI: Pleasant Company Publications.

References

Madison, L. (2002). *The feelings book: The care & keeping of your emotions.* Middleton, WI: Pleasant Company Publications.

Mazur, B. (2009, May 29). *What should a professional mathematician know?* Retrieved from http://www.math.harvard.edu/~mazur/preprints/math_ed_2.pdf.

Myles, B., Endow, J., & Mayfield, M. (2013). *The hidden curriculum of getting and keeping a job: Navigating the social landscape of employment. A guide for individuals with autism spectrum and other social-cognitive challenges.* Shawnee Mission, KS: AAPC Publishing.

Myles, H. M., & Kolar, A. (2013). *The hidden curriculum and other practical solutions to everyday challenges for elementary-age children with high-functioning autism spectrum disorders* (2nd ed.). Shawnee Mission, KS: AAPC Publishing.

National Autism Center (NAC). (2009). *National standards report: Addressing the need for evidence-based practice guidelines for autism spectrum disorders.* Randolph, MA: Author. Retrieved from http://www.nationalautismcenter.org/nsp.

National Professional Development Center on Autism Spectrum Disorders. (NPDC on ASD). (n.d.). *Evidence based practice briefs.* Retrieved from http://autismpdc.fpg.unc.edu/content/briefs.

Packer, A. J. (1992). *Bringing up parents: The teenager's handbook.* Minneapolis, MN: Free Spirit Publishing Inc.

Packer, A. J. (1997). *How rude! The teenager's guide to good manners, proper behavior, and not grossing people out.* Minneapolis, MN: Free Spirit Publishing Inc.

Plunkett, K., & Juola, P. (1999). A connectionist model of English past tense and plural morphology. *Cognitive Science, 23*(4), 463-490.

Raymer, D. (2002). *Staying home alone: A girl's guide to feeling safe and having fun.* Middleton, WI: Pleasant Company Publications.

Schaefer, V. L. (1998). *The care & keeping of you: The body book for girls.* Middleton, WI: Pleasant Company Publications.

Test, D. W., Mazzotti, V. L., Mustian, A. L., Fowler, C. H., Kortering, L, & Kohler, P. (2009). Evidence-based secondary transition predictors for improving postschool outcomes for students with disabilities. *Career Development for Exceptional Individuals, 32*, 160-181.

Advance Praise

"What an invaluable resource for family members, service providers, and friends supporting individuals who have difficulty navigating the unwritten rules of different environments and who struggle with everyday social situations. This is your 'go-to' resource! The short vignettes provided throughout each chapter allow readers to understand the true complexity of the 'hidden curriculum.' Quick to read, yet filled with examples and practical tips for addressing and teaching the 'hidden curriculum,' this is one book that you will definitely recommend to others. Enjoy!
–   Amy Bixler Coffin, MS, Autism Center program director, Ohio Center for Autism and Low Incidence; co-author, *Out and About: Preparing Children With Autism Spectrum Disorders to Participate in Their Communities*

"This remarkable guidebook is invaluable for helping persons with social-cognitive difficulties make sense of unspoken rules and expectations that govern how we interact with others in everyday life. In a well-written, straightforward and friendly style, the authors provide excellent insights and sensible tools that draw from a wealth of research and experience. *The Hidden Curriculum* is sure to rank high on my list of recommended resources."
– Pamela Wolfberg, PhD, San Francisco State University & Autism Institute on Peer Relations and Play; author, *Peer Play and the Autism Spectrum: The Art of Guiding Children's Socialization and Imagination*

"*The Hidden Curriculum* clarifies exactly what cues and mores are 'invisible' to us who have Asperger Syndrome and related disorders. In addition to individuals who have social-cognitive disorders, this is a recommended read for every muggle, excuse me, non-autistic person, who interacts with those of us on the autism spectrum."
– Jennifer McIlwee Myers, "Aspie-at-Large"

About the Authors

Brenda Smith Myles, PhD, a consultant with the Ohio Center for Autism and Low Incidence (OCALI) and the Ziggurat Group, is the recipient of the Autism Society of America's Outstanding Professional Award, the Princeton Fellowship Award, and the Council for Exceptional Children, Division on Developmental Disabilities Burton Blatt Humanitarian Award. Brenda has made over 1,000 presentations all over the world and written more than 200 articles and books on ASD. In addition, she served as the co-chair of the National ASD Teacher Standards Committee; was on the National Institute of Mental Health's Interagency Autism Coordinating Committee's Strategic Planning Consortium; and collaborated with the National Professional Center on Autism Spectrum Disorders, National Autism Center, and the Centers for Medicare and Medicaid Services who identified evidence-based practices for individuals with autism spectrum disorders and served as project director for the Texas Autism Resource Guide for Teachers (TARGET). Myles is also on the executive boards of several organizations, including the Scientific Council of the Organization for Autism Research (SCORE) and ASTEP – Asperger Syndrome Training and Education Program. Further, in the latest survey conducted by the University of Texas, she was acknowledged as the second most productive applied researcher in ASD in the world.

Melissa L. Trautman, MSEd, is a special education teacher with several years of experience working with children with autism spectrum disorders. She is the author of *My New School: A Workbook to Help Students Transition to a New School* and co-author of the *2011 One-a-Day Hidden Curriculum Calendar for Children*.

Ronda L. Schelvan, MS, has worked for more than 30 years in the field of special education, including extensive experience working/supporting students and families with special needs. She has presented and consulted nationally and internationally. In addition to serving as co-chair of Southwest Washington's Autism Consulting Cadre for 10 years, Ronda collaborated on the Autism Guidebook for Washington State. She has served as past president of the Southwest Washington Chapter of the Autism Society of Washington. Ronda also teaches classes and serves as a mentor for the Autism Outreach Project of Washington. Currently, she teaches for the Evergreen School District in Vancouver, Washington.

WITHDRAWN

P.O. Box 23173
Shawnee Mission, Kansas 66283-0173
www.aapcpublishing.net

CPSIA information can be obtained at www.ICGtesting.com
Printed in the USA
LVOW101540300613

340852LV00003B/3/P

9 781937 473747